The New Scribner Music Library

DR. HOWARD HANSON

EDITOR-IN-CHIEF

VOLUME 11

Reference Volume

CHARLES SCRIBNER'S SONS · NEW YORK

13 15 17 19 21 23 25 27 29 MO/C 30 28 26 24 22 20 18 16 14

PRINTED IN THE UNITED STATES OF AMERICA

SBN 684-13112-9 (Index)

SBN 684-13100-5 (Vols. 1-10 with Reference Volume, including Index)

Contents

The Volumes

VOLUME 1
"Easy Piano Music by American Composers"
Editor: Dr. Merle Montgomery

VOLUME 2
"Keyboard Panorama"
Editor: Blanche Winogron

VOLUME 3
"Piano Classics"
Editor: Blanche Winogron

VOLUME 4
"A Century Of Piano Music"
Editor: Dr. Merle Montgomery

VOLUME 5
"All-Time Piano Favorites"
Editor: Dr. Ruth Watanabe

VOLUME 6
"Piano Music for Two"
Editor: Dr. Ruth Watanabe

VOLUME 7
"At the Opera"
Editor: Dr. David Russell Williams

VOLUME 8
"Music for the Dance"
Editor: Dr. Ruth Watanabe

VOLUME 9
"Home Favorites"
Editor: Philip L. Miller

VOLUME 10
"Art Songs"
Editor: Philip L. Miller

VOLUME 11
"Reference Volume"

Publisher's Preface

WHAT IS
THE NEW SCRIBNER MUSIC LIBRARY?

THE NEW SCRIBNER MUSIC LIBRARY consists of ten volumes of piano and vocal music and one Reference Volume (Volume 11)—a total of over 2,700 pages offering nearly 1,000 pieces by close to 350 composers. In addition, the Reference Volume presents a detailed *Biographical Dictionary* of the composers represented in THE NEW SCRIBNER MUSIC LIBRARY, a *Dictionary of Musical Terms*, and a *Pictorial History of Keyboard Instruments and Keyboard Music*. It also contains a complete *Index* to all the compositions contained in the ten music volumes, arranged by composers, as well as by titles.

OVER-ALL STRUCTURE

The ten music volumes of THE NEW SCRIBNER MUSIC LIBRARY are organized as follows: while each of the volumes is a self-contained unit, together they provide a uniquely comprehensive coverage of all keyboard music from its beginnings until today, as well as a generous sampling of vocal music, from folksongs and hymns to recital songs and opera excerpts. There are no musical duplications from volume to volume; the volumes complement each other; each highlights a different aspect of the total complex of the keyboard and vocal music of our Western civilization.

AMERICAN MUSIC

One unusual feature of THE NEW SCRIBNER MUSIC LIBRARY worth singling out is its special emphasis of America's creative efforts in the field of music. For example, an entire volume (Volume 1) is devoted exclusively to easy piano pieces by American composers, a total of 201 teaching pieces, most of them written specifically for this volume and never before published. In addition, thirty fully professional compositions by twenty-one distinguished American composers are contained in Volume 4 (for detailed descriptions of the individual volumes see below). Most of these latter pieces, too, were specially commissioned for THE NEW SCRIBNER MUSIC LIBRARY and are published here for the first time. Still other American music appears in several of the remaining volumes, including American home and folksongs, spirituals, hymns, and art songs.

EDITORIAL STAFF

In addition to the over-all direction by the editor-in-chief, Dr. Howard Hanson, five distinguished specialists were appointed to compile and edit the individual volumes, in order to insure the broadest possible spectrum of musical, educational, and music-editorial approaches. These special editors are Philip L. Miller, Dr. Merle Montgomery, Dr. Ruth Watanabe, Blanche Winogron, and Dr. David Russell Williams.

The publishers of THE NEW SCRIBNER MUSIC LIBRARY, Charles Scribner's Sons, in turn, appointed Kurt Stone, one of America's most experienced administrative editors in the music publishing field, as Project Coordinator and Managing Editor.

GRADINGS

The range of technical difficulty throughout THE NEW SCRIBNER MUSIC LIBRARY extends from the easy piano pieces of Volume 1 and the simple folksongs and hymns of Volume 9, to the mature keyboard works by the foremost composers of the Baroque, Classical, Romantic, and 20th-century eras, and the corresponding art songs and operatic arias. In addition, Volume 6 is devoted entirely to four-hand pieces, and Volume 1 also contains a number of simple piano duets.

PERFORMANCE AIDS

Almost all of the non-vocal music in THE NEW SCRIBNER MUSIC LIBRARY has been supplied with fingerings.

Care has also been taken to insure good, practical page-turns throughout the volumes. Similarly, the staff and note sizes never go beyond the limits of maximum efficiency and legibility. There are no unwieldy jumbo notes for simple music, nor are the notes of the vocal accompaniments and operatic piano reductions smaller than in normal piano music.

HISTORICAL COVERAGE

The earliest composition contained in THE NEW SCRIBNER MUSIC LIBRARY dates back to about 1350, while the most recent pieces are of our own time—many of them published here first.

NATIONALITIES

While THE NEW SCRIBNER MUSIC LIBRARY includes an unusually high percentage of music from our own country and our neighbors north and south, fourteen European countries are also represented, as well as Japan.

MUSICAL FORMS AND TYPES

PIANO MUSIC—THE NEW SCRIBNER MUSIC LIBRARY covers the entire range of the literature for solo piano (and earlier keyboard instruments), from short songs and dance movements to Beethoven sonatas, from Baroque chorale preludes and Bach *Inventions* to preludes and fugues, from suites and sets of variations to descriptive pieces of the Romantic era, from salon and ballet music, waltzes, and marches to free forms, large and small, from all periods. In addition, numerous original piano duets (four-hand pieces) of all forms and in all degrees of difficulty are provided.

VOCAL MUSIC—Apart from the home and folksongs, hymns, spirituals, and children's songs, etc., already mentioned, THE NEW SCRIBNER MUSIC LIBRARY presents an entire volume (Volume 10) of art songs, from the earliest manifestations, through numerous songs by the greatest song composers of all: Schubert, Schumann, Brahms, and Wolf, to recital songs of our own time, including works by Benjamin Britten, Aaron Copland, Igor Stravinsky, and many other 20th-century composers.—All songs with foreign-language texts also have singable English translations, many of which were especially prepared for THE NEW SCRIBNER MUSIC LIBRARY.

OPERA—Twelve famous operas have been excerpted to provide a historical survey of operatic music (Volume 7).

The survey begins with early pioneer works by Monteverdi and Purcell, continues with the most celebrated masterworks—*Orpheus* (Gluck), *Figaro* (Mozart), *Tristan, Parsifal, Aida, Faust, Carmen,* and Mussorgsky's *Boris Godunov*—and finally leads to the more recent *La Bohème* and to Debussy's *Pelléas and Mélisande.*—As in the art-song volume, all operas in foreign languages also have singable English texts. Besides, each of the sets of excerpts is preceded by a synopsis of the respective plot.

BIOGRAPHICAL INFORMATION

The detailed *Biographical Reference Dictionary* of the composers represented in THE NEW SCRIBNER MUSIC LIBRARY was specially prepared by the eminent lexicographer Nicolas Slonimsky, and includes information that has come to light only now and is not yet available in any other biographical dictionaries.

PICTORIAL HISTORY OF KEYBOARD INSTRUMENTS

The *Pictorial History of Keyboard Instruments and Keyboard Music* was prepared by the Managing Editor of THE NEW SCRIBNER MUSIC LIBRARY, Kurt Stone. It ranges from early clavichords, virginals, and chamber organs, via harpsichords and early pianos, to present-day instruments, and includes facsimile reproductions of musical manuscripts or early published editions of keyboard music or recital songs hailing from the same periods as the instruments shown. Wherever possible, the facsimile reproductions are of compositions also contained in the main body of THE NEW SCRIBNER MUSIC LIBRARY.

GLOSSARY

The *Reference Dictionary of Musical Terms* was prepared by Nicolas Slonimsky.

A
BRIEF
PICTORIAL HISTORY
of
KEYBOARD INSTRUMENTS
and
KEYBOARD MUSIC

by
Kurt Stone

Introductory Note

The following illustrations are limited to home instruments. Thus the most majestic keyboard instrument, the church organ, is not included, nor are keyboard instruments chiefly used in the orchestra.

The oldest instruments shown date back to the sixteenth century, even though key-operated organs (with few tones) were already known in ancient Greece (the *hydraulis*), and the earliest stringed instruments with keys, essentially clavichords, date back to the eleven-hundreds.

By the middle of the fourteenth century, organs as well as clavichords had developed sufficiently to cause the emergence of a regular keyboard literature, such as the music in the so-called *Robertsbridge Codex,* of which an example will be found on page 9 of Volume 2 of *The New Scribner Music Library.*

Harpsichords came later—the earliest instruments date back to ca. 1400. Their tone was louder and more brilliant than the intimate and quiet tone of the clavichord, since the strings of a harpsichord are plucked, rather than gently struck. To add to their brilliance and to create great timbral variety, several sets of strings soon were built into the harpsichord, which could be played separately or together, and two keyboards instead of one were built to add even greater contrasts. (Our illustrations include one of the rare instruments with *three* keyboards.)

Then, in the early seventeen-hundreds, the pianoforte was invented. Its strings were no longer plucked, but struck with padded hammers. Gradually, the piano (as we now call it) gained in popularity and began to replace the clavichord and harpsichord, until during the last 150 years or so, it has reigned supreme. Its tone quality, however, changed considerably over the years: early pianos—those of Haydn's and Mozart's days—were very close in sound to the harpsichord. Their tone was clear, thin, delicate, with sharp attacks. As music grew smoother, more personal, more harmony-oriented during the Romantic and Impressionist eras, the piano sound also grew smoother and more voluptuous. Besides, the mechanism of the piano developed from its rather crude beginnings to an almost miraculous sensitivity and efficiency.

The sound of the organ had a similar development. The early organs of the Renaissance and Baroque were bright and clear, each stop had a character of its own, and the attacks were pointed up by a short, initial air-sound, the *chif.* With the growing reflectiveness and emotionalism of the music of the late Classical and Romantic eras, organ sound also changed to blend more harmoniously, rather than to contrast. Organs now began to emulate the orchestra, thereby losing some of their former individuality. Small home organs could not measure up to these demands and were soon replaced by the reed organ or *harmonium,* and the sharply defined tone colors of organ polyphony were replaced by the swelling and fading of lush blends of sound.

Our own era is characterized by two musical trends pointing in opposite directions. On the one hand, we have re-discovered the music of earlier times, and with this rediscovery have revived the instruments for which it was written. Thus we are building clavichords, harpsichords, and small pipe organs again. On the other hand, we have entered into the fascinating field of new sounds and sound-producing systems. The electronic organ has already replaced the reed organ, and the most recent, purely electronic sound-generators with their immense and unprecedented versatility are on the rise everywhere. Even so, the piano continues to be the unchallenged queen of home instruments.

K.S.

The Two Most Important Small Stringed
Keyboard Instruments of the Past

THE CLAVICHORD

2. Italian Spinet, built in Venice in 1540.

(The Metropolitan Museum of Art; Joseph Pulitzer Bequest, 1953.)

A Spinet is a small harpsichord having only one set of strings. This particular instrument is extra small, for which reason it is called a Spinettino. It sounds one octave higher than a normal-sized instrument. (See Fig. 10.)

◀ **1. German Clavichord, built 1765 by John Christopher Jesse.**

(The Metropolitan Museum of Art; Gift of Mrs. John Crosby Brown, 1889.)

Note that the keys are suspended freely, without a keybed under them. When a key is depressed, a small metal prong or *tangent*, mounted on the far end of the key, rises vertically until it hits and presses against the string. It is this contact with the string, rather than a keybed below the key, that stops the key. (See Fig. 3.)

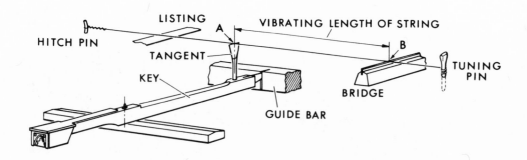

3. Clavichord Action.

In this drawing, the key has been depressed, so that the metal "tangent" at the far end of the key is pressing up against the string, acting as a temporary bridge in that it divides the string into two segments. The left segment is damped by the "listing," while the right segment (between A and B) vibrates. As soon as the key is released, the tangent no longer divides the string, whereupon the listing silences the entire string.

4. Harpsichord Action.

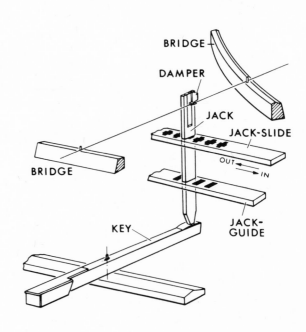

When the key is depressed, it pushes up the jack which has a thorn-like plectrum of quill or leather (though now-a-days usually of plastic). The plectrum plucks the string when passing it, while the damper at the top of the jack is raised, permitting the string to vibrate. When the key is released, the jack falls back (the plectrum recedes, so as not to touch the string when passing it downward), and the damper comes to rest on the string, silencing it. Harpsichords have one to three sets of strings to each keyboard, and one to three jacks to each key. Each set of jacks (called a stop) produces a different timbre, loudness, and/or octave. The jack-slides add or subtract sets of jacks at the discretion of the player, by moving them toward the strings or away from them.—Spinets have no jack-slides because they have only a single set of jacks.

(Both drawings reprinted by permission of Harvard Dictionary of Music, 2nd Edition, by Willi Apel, Cambridge, The Belknap Press of Harvard University Press. Copyright © 1944, 1969, by the President and Fellows of Harvard College.)

5. Inside view of a Clavichord, built in Germany in the first half of the 18th century.

(The Metropolitan Museum of Art; The Crosby Brown Collection of Musical Instruments, 1889.)

Note the strange angles of the keys, necessary to strike each string at a point best suited to produce the correct pitch. The damping material (called listing) is actually woven around all the strings.

6. Flemish Double Virginal, built by Hans Ruckers in Antwerp, 1581.
(The Metropolitan Museum of Art; Gift of B. H. Homan, 1929.)
The next best thing to a two-manual harpsichord (see Fig. 13) was to have two spinets in one. The left keyboard acts on the short strings of the small slide-box to which it belongs; it is pitched one octave higher than normal. The right keyboard belongs to the case proper and plays the long strings at normal pitch. In England, the term virginal or virginals was preferred to spinet; we speak of the English virginalists, never spinettists. The origin of the term "virginal" is not clear. It may have come from the Latin *virga,* meaning rod, another name for the jacks.

7. Detail of the painting inside the lid of the same instrument.

8. Facsimile reproduction of the manuscript of *A Gigge. Doctor Bull's my selfe*, by John Bull, as it appears in the Fitzwilliam Virginal Book, a large collection of English keyboard music from the late sixteenth century and now in the Fitzwilliam Museum in Cambridge, England.

10. English Spinet, built by Thomas Hitchcock, ca. 1700.
(The Metropolitan Museum of Art; Gift of Joseph W. Drexel, 1889.)
A full-size spinet. Note the jack-rail which runs parallel to the keyboard. It prevents the jacks from being propelled too high.

◀ **9. A literal transcription of the beginning of the Gigge into modern notation,** reprinted from the Fitzwilliam Virginal Book as edited by J. A. Fuller Maitland and W. Barklay Squire (1899). (The piece appears in its entirety on page 18 of Volume 2 of *The New Scribner Music Library.*)

Note that the time-signature "3" is out in the left margin, and that unstemmed black notes are used for half-notes and stemmed ones for quarters. (Dotted half-notes in this kind of triple meter were written as stemmed open notes, like our undotted half-notes, but in the example, the open note-heads have filled in.) The staves have six lines; the upper staff is in G-clef, the lower in Bass clef. At the extreme right of each staff is a small warning sign or *custos* for each voice, "previewing" the first note of the following line.

11. Facsimile reproduction of J. S. Bach's manuscript (1722) of the Fugue No. 2 in C minor from The Well-Tempered Clavier, Volume I. (It appears on page 22 of Volume 3 of *The New Scribner Music Library.*)

The term "Clavier" was used loosely in Bach's time; it meant no more than "Keyboard," and the performer chose from among available instruments—clavichord, spinet, harpsichord, or organ—according to the structure or character of the music. (The often encountered translation "Well-Tempered Clavichord" for *Das Wohltem-perierte Clavier* is incorrect.)

Note that the vertical rhythmic alignment of the notes, which had looked rather confusing in the piece by John Bull (Fig. 8) is now, some 120 years later, straightened out, and that Bach uses a five-line staff instead of Bull's six lines, but that he notates the right hand in a C-clef. He still adheres to the tradition of the *custos*.

12. Italian Harpsichord with One Manual, probably from the Seventeenth Century. The paintings in the lid are assumed to be by Gaspard Dughet (1613-1675).

(The Metropolitan Museum of Art; Gift of Susan Dwight Bliss, 1945.)

Other commonly encountered names for the harpsichord are clavicembalo, gravicembalo, and cembalo.

13. Flemish Harpsichord with Two Manuals, built ca. 1650 by Joannes Couchet.

(Figs. 13-15: The Metropolitan Museum of Art; The Crosby Brown Collection of Musical Instruments, 1889.)

The case of this harpsichord is decorated with carvings and gilt gesso work. The buttons for changing the stops protrude from the right-hand side of the case (see close-up on next page). Music of the Baroque era—the era of the harpsichord—is characterized by *contrasts* in trimbre and/or loudness, rather than by *gradual* transitions of crescendo and diminuendo. The two keyboards make possible rapid changes from one set of strings or combination of strings to another, as well as a clear separation of different parts.

15. This close-up shows the jacks with the jack rails removed for better visibility. On the side of the case are the obviously much-used stops which were pulled out or pushed in, thus moving the connected jack-slides and their respective jacks away or toward the strings. The strings reaching all the way to the keyboard are longer than the others: the long ones sound at normal pitch (called 8-foot, a term borrowed from organ stops), while the short ones sound one octave higher (4-foot). The fourth stop is a "Lute"—it damps the strings while they are played, producing a lute-like sound.

14. This close-up of the manuals also shows the two jack-rails and the jacks (behind the keys and the first row of tuning pins), as well as the rose in the sounding board.

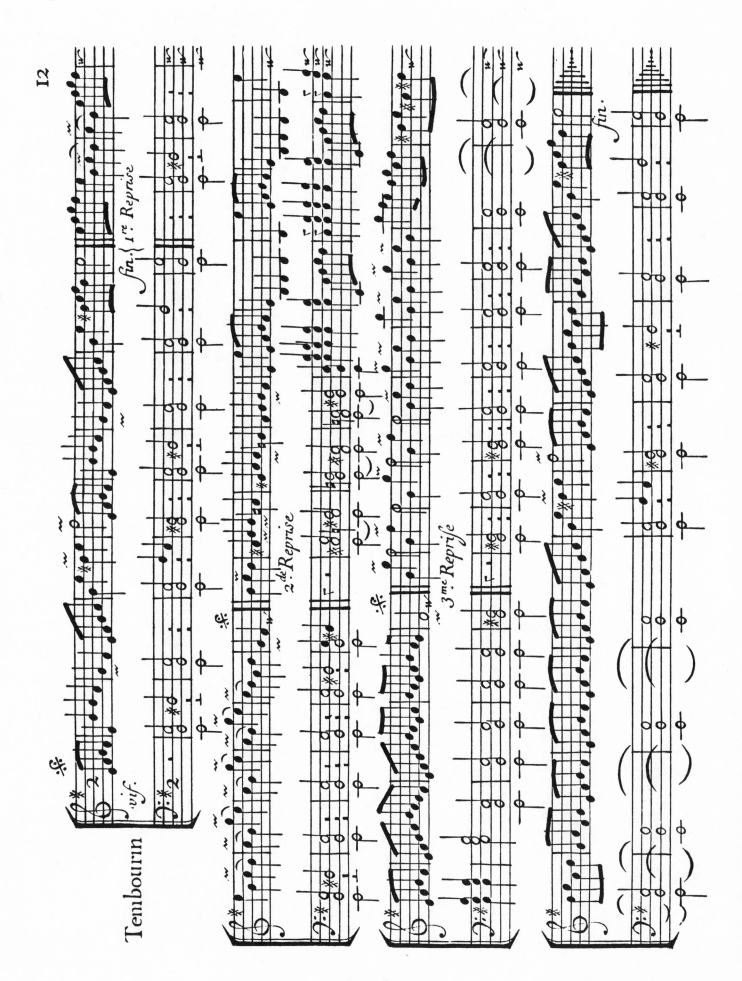

17. Italian Upright Harpsichord, called a Clavicytherium or Clavicembalo verticale, built in the early sixteenhundreds.

(The Metropolitan Museum of Art; The Crosby Brown Collection of Musical Instruments, 1889.)

◀ **16. Facsimile reproduction of "*Tembourin*" by Jean-Philippe Rameau, from *Pièces de Clavessin*, published in Paris in 1724.** (It appears on page 118 of Volume 2 of *The New Scribner Music Library*, where it is properly called *Le Tambourin*.)

In the days of the late Baroque, French music was considered more modern than the music of the Germans. This newness even shows in the notation. In our example, the right hand is notated in G-clef instead of in C-clef, and we even find a curious notational innovation (that did *not* survive): in the first four measures of the 3*me.* *Reprise*, half-notes straddle the barlines instead of being broken up into two tied quarter-notes. Not everything is new, however. Each voice still has its *custos* (see Figs. 8 and 12) at the end of the line.

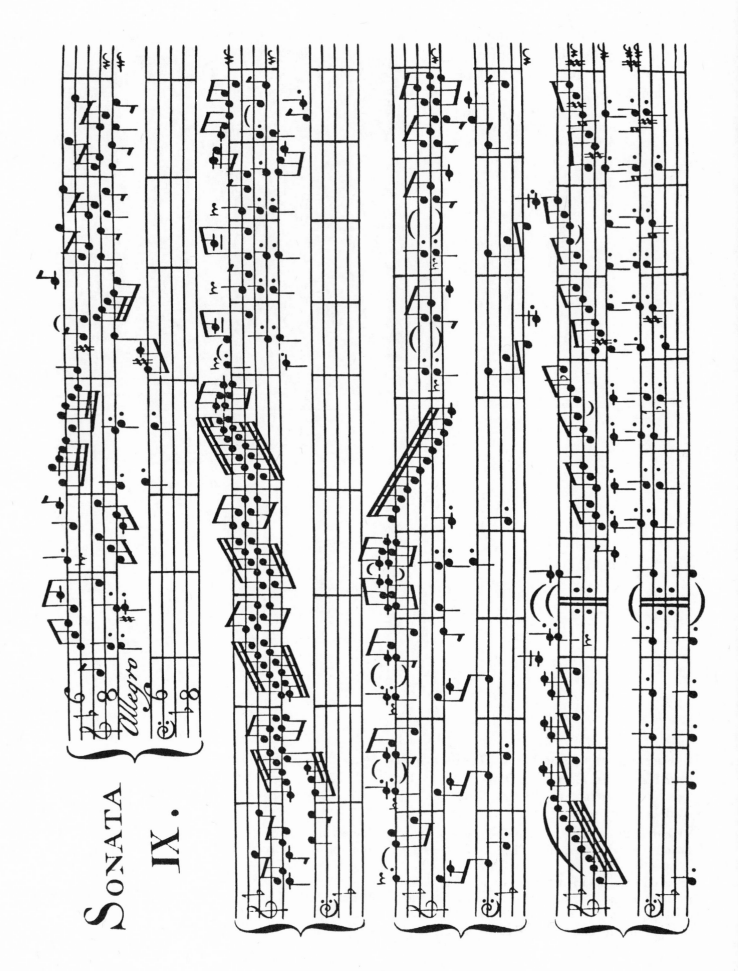

19. Italian Harpsichord with Three Manuals, built by Vincenze Sodi in Florence, 1779.

(The Metropolitan Museum of Art; The Crosby Brown Collection of Musical Instruments, 1889.)

Harpsichords with three manuals were extremely rare. Strangely enough, this particular instrument has no stops; none of the three manuals permits any variation of timbre.

◀ **18. Facsimile reproduction of *Sonata No. IX* by Domenico Scarlatti, from *Essercizi per Gravicembalo*, published in 1738.** (It appears on page 129 of Volume 2 of *The New Scribner Music Library* under the title by which it is commonly known: *Sonata "Pastorale."*)

This example shows an interesting notational problem: since the music roams unusually freely over the entire compass of the keyboard, one would either have to alternate frequently between Bass clef and G-clef in order to keep the left-hand notes in the lower staff, or one would have to disregard separating the hands by staves and put the notes wherever they fit best. This first edition follows the latter course.

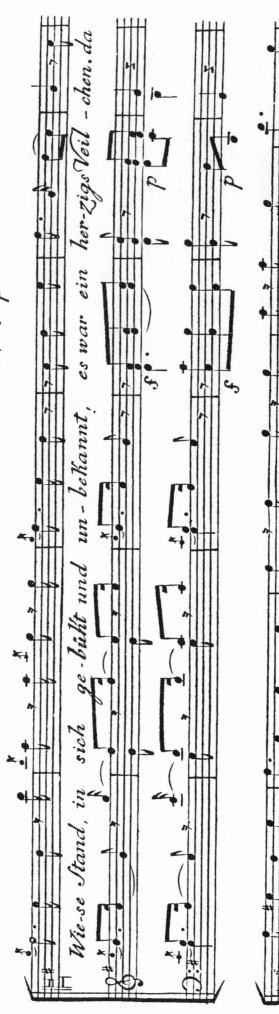

21. *Piano Forte,* **built by Cristofori in Florence, 1720.**

(The Metropolitan Museum of Art; The Crosby Brown Collection of Musical Instruments, 1889.)

In the early seventeen-hundreds, Bartolomeo Christofori (1655-1731), a celebrated builder of harpsichords, replaced the harpsichord's jacks and their plectra with small hammers that *struck* the strings from below instead of plucking them. He thus became the inventor of the piano.

Note the similarity in shape of the early piano and the harpsichord. There even is a wooden slat that looks like the jack-rail; it keeps the dampers from jumping too high during loud passages. Note also that there are no pedals as yet.

20. Facsimile reproduction of the famous song *Das Veilchen (The Violet)* **by Wolfgang Amadeus Mozart, in its first edition by Artaria, Vienna 1789.** (It appears on page 144 of Volume 10 of *The New Scribner Music Library.*)

The Baroque era is gone; subjective expressivity has come. Note the relatively great number of phrasing slurs and dynamic indications. There are even staccato wedges on the sixteenth-notes! The right hand is notated in G-clef, while the voice is in Soprano clef, a C-clef on the first staff line. (Vocal parts above the Bass voice continued to be notated in the traditional C-clefs all the way through Brahms and beyond.)

22. English Square Piano, built by Johannes Zumpe in London, 1761.
(The Metropolitan Museum of Art; The Crosby Brown Collection of Musical Instruments, 1889.)
It was a long time until pianos found their own, intrinsic shapes. At first sight, this instrument could easily be mistaken for a clavichord or spinet.

23. American Square Piano, built by John Tallman in New York, 1825.
(The Metropolitan Museum of Art; The Crosby Brown Collection of Musical Instruments, 1889.)
At first, the square shape was the most popular for pianos. It was more practical as a piece of furniture than the wing-shaped piano, and it also was cheaper to build. The latter consideration, however, did not preclude the creation of luxury models, such as shown here. Its mahogany case is profuse with gilt decorations, not to mention the carved feet, the center lyre, and the massive horizontal and vertical supports. This instrument also has two pedals.

24-25. A "Work-Box Piano" (closed and open) by an unknown European maker, probably early 19th century.

(The Metropolitan Museum of Art; The Crosby Brown Collection of Musical Instruments, 1889.)

Once the piano as such was firmly established, it was built in untold shapes and guises. This particular instrument, closed, looks like a sewing table, and indeed it is (note the lids for the yarn and needle receptacles). The back of the music rack doubles as a mirror.

26. Dutch Giraffe Piano, built by Van der Hoef in Amsterdam in the early eighteen-hundreds.

(Victoria and Albert Museum, London.)

A popular forerunner of the "upright" was the giraffe piano. Its shape permitted the low strings to have the proper length for a good, full tone, a characteristic sadly missing in today's mini pianos (see Figs. 40 and 41). As our illustration shows, giraffes also lent themselves to great feats of decorative art.

Piano-Forte.

SOUVENIR de la POLOGNE.

EIGHT MAZURKAS, Composed by FRED. CHOPIN.

Nº 2. Op: 7.

Dedicated to Monsieur Johns, de la Nouvelle Orleans.

Legato   (W & Cº Nº 959.)

28. Steinway Grand Piano, built in 1859.

(Illustration courtesy of Steinway & Sons.)

The firm of Steinway & Sons was established in New York in 1853 by the members of the Steinway family, who had begun to move from Germany to the US in 1849.

Our illustration shows that they were no novices at building pianos. It also shows that they were entirely in tune with the cravings of their time for decorative lavishness, even though the way in which they utilized the beautiful natural designs of the wood grain far outshines the rather gaudy sumptuousness of the carvings.

◀ **27. Facsimile reproduction of the Mazurka in B-flat Major, Opus 7 No. 1, by Frédéric Chopin, as published in 1839(?) by Wessel & Co., London, *Importers & Publishers of Foreign Music (by special Appointment) to H.R.H. the Duchess of Kent.*** (It appears on page 212 of Volume 2 of *The New Scribner Music Library*.)

Chopin published his early works with opus numbers which often differ from those by which the pieces are known to us. These early numbers usually reflect the order of publication, while the later ones reflect the order of composition.— Note the British form of the quarter-rests in measures 12 and 15, and in the upbeat to the second part (all in the left hand). They are mirror images of eighth-rests.

29-30. Facsimile reproduction of the title page and first page of music of the first edition of *Old Folks at Home* by Stephen C. Foster, published by Firth, Pond & Co., New York, in 1851. (The song appears in a slightly different form on page 91 of Volume 9 of *The New Scribner Music Library*)

This famous song has had a strange history. When Foster began to write what he called "Ethiopian" songs, he did not want to use his own name because he was not sure how the public would react. He therefore made an agreement with E. P. Christy of Christy's Minstrels to publish the first edition of *Old Folks at Home* under Christy's name (see the reproduction). When the song (and others in the same style) grew exceedingly popular, Foster wanted his name on the music after all and wrote to Christy to this effect on May 25, 1852, but now Christy seems to have balked, because a copy of 1854, marked "Fiftieth Edition," and a re-issue by Oliver Ditson Co. of 1873, still only list Christy's name as lyricist and composer.

[36]

OLD FOLKS AT HOME

Words and Music by E. P. CHRISTY.

Way down upon de Swanee ribber, Far, far a——way,

Dere's wha my heart is turning ebber, Dere's wha de old folks stay.

1333

31. South German Chamber Organ, built in 1758.

(The Metropolitan Museum of Art; The Crosby Brown Collection of Musical Instruments, 1889.)

In our time, pipe organs are used almost exclusively in churches and in large concert halls, but in the days of the Renaissance and Baroque, organs were found everywhere and they were of all sizes. Those that could be transported easily were called Portatives; slightly larger ones were called Positive Organs. The positive organ here illustrated has one manual with two stops, and no pedal keyboard. It is a very late representative of this type of organ.

32. Hamilton Reed Organ, built by Baldwin in the early nineteen-hundreds.

(Illustration courtesy of the Baldwin Piano & Organ Company.)

Reed organs were invented in the beginning of the 19th century and quickly replaced the small pipe organs in the home. Their tone is produced by metal tongues (reeds) which are caused to vibrate by means of air streams. There are many different types of reed organs (or *harmoniums*), each with a host of special attachments for making musical performances more effective. Some of these permit octave doublings of the top tones of chords, while others stress their bass tones or bring out the melody. There are gadgets that produce sharp, instant attacks of tones with the help of small hammers; there are vibrato and tremolo buttons and swells, and there are many different stops bearing promising, evocative names, though they all sound disappointingly similar. In some instruments, key pressure will affect loudness. Air is usually pumped by the player with the help of treadles, and knee-levers often operate shutter mechanisms for swelling and fading, as well as pre-set crescendo effects.

THE PARLOR ORGAN

(REED ORGAN)

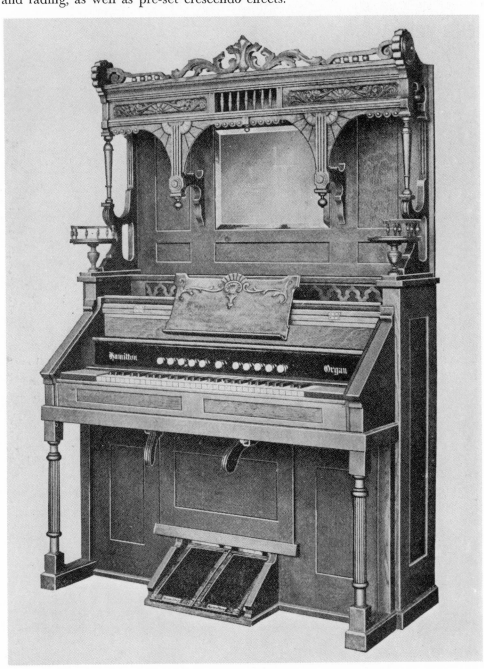

33. Baldwin Parlor Organ, Model 126

(Illustration courtesy of the Baldwin Piano & Organ Company.)

Small organs working on electricity have replaced the reed organ. They are immensely versatile. Their stops consist of pre-set imitations of instruments, from saxophones to trombones, from harps and guitars to vibraphones, flutes, string instruments, clarinets, practically anything. In fact, the model shown even has facilities for mixing one's own sounds: an adaptation of the synthesizer (see Fig. 44). In addition there are vibrato and tremolo effects, arpeggios, and echoes. There also are pre-selected chord progressions suitable for simple accompaniments; they play continuously in a whole array of different rhythms. Simulated drum sounds also come in continuous rhythms of many kinds. And as an added convenience, the organ here shown has an attachment for tapes and cassettes, and for recording one's own performances.

34. A Modern Steinway Grand

(Illustration courtesy of Steinway & Sons.)

The modern grand is the crowning glory of piano history. Its shape is elegant, its action is ingenious and remarkably reliable, its compass far exceeds that of all other instruments, save the organ. Its sound is rich and versatile, its dynamics range from a pianissimo whisper to a thunderous fortissimo. The longer the strings, the better the sound. A concert grand may be as long as 9 feet and more. Our illustration shows a medium sized instrument, ideally suited for home use.

THE MODERN GRAND

35. The Precision Work of the Key-to-Hammer Action of a Steinway Grand.

36. The Action Explained.
(Both illustrations courtesy of Steinway & Sons.)

Cross section of grand piano action: 1. Keybed. 2. Keyframe. 3. Front rail. 4. Balance rail. 5. Balance rail stud. 6. Back rail. 7. Key stop rail. 8. White key. 9. Key covering. 10. Black key. 11. Key button. 12. Backcheck. 13. Underlever key cushion. 14. Action hanger. 15. Support rail. 16. Support. 17. Fly. 18. Support top flange. 19. Balancer. 20. Repetition spring. 21. Hammer rest. 22. Regulating rail. 23. Hammer rail. 24. Hammershank. 25. Hammer. 26. Underlever frame. 27. Underlever. 28. Damper stop rail. 29. Damper wire. 30. Damper guide rail. 31. Damper head. 32. Damper felts. 33. String. 34. Tuning pin. 35. Sostenuto rod. (Courtesy of Steinway & Sons.)

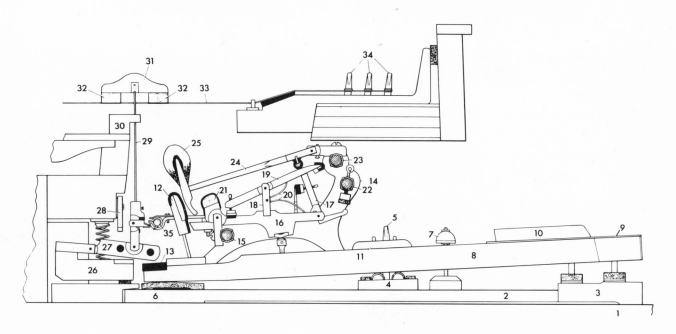

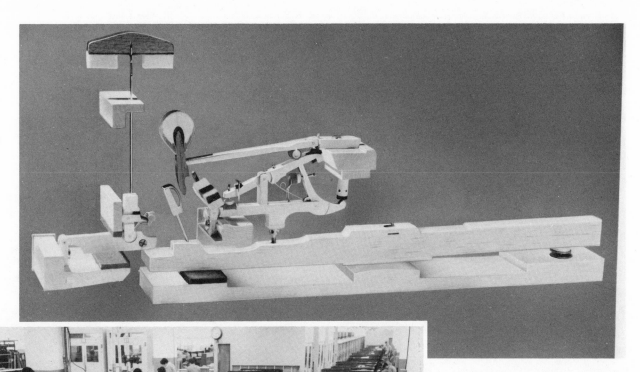

37. The Precision Work of the Key-to-Hammer Action in a Yamaha Piano.

(Illustration courtesy of George Krippenstapel, piano historian, and reproduced by permission of Yamaha International Corp., California.)

38-39. Assembly Line and Check-Out Hall at the Yamaha Piano Plant.

(Illustrations courtesy of George Krippenstapel, piano historian, and reproduced by permission of Yamaha International Corp., California.)

40. Small Modern Vertical Piano—the 36-inch Baldwin.

(Illustration courtesy of the Baldwin Piano & Organ Company.)

Today's typical urban living conditions—small rooms in small apartments—demand small pieces of furniture. As a result, pianos have been "miniaturized," unfortunately to a slight impairment of their tone quality. Naturally, it is impossible for a small piano to have strings long enough to produce the full, rich sound of a concert grand.

41. Inside Views of the Vertical Piano Shown in Fig. 40.

(Illustration courtesy of the Baldwin Piano & Organ Company.)

Note the ingenious arrangement of the strings: they run diagonally so that they can be as long as possible. At the same time, their playing points are in the proper positions for the hammers to strike them.

42. A Neupert Spinet, Model "Silbermann."

(Illustration courtesy of Magnamusic Distributors, Inc., Sharon, Conn., USA Representatives of J. C. Neupert.)

This modern spinet has one 8-foot stop and a divided Lute (see Fig. 15) which damps either the upper or the lower strings or *all* strings, as desired.

REVIVAL OF THE PAST

43. A Neupert Harpsichord, Model "Corelli."

(Illustration courtesy of Magnamusic Distributors, Inc., Sharon, Conn., USA Representatives of J. C. Neupert.)

A modern harpsichord with two manuals. The stops (two 8-foot stops and one 4-foot) are operated with pedals instead of by hand as in the old instruments (see Fig. 15). A hand button for the Lute stop appears above the upper manual on the left.

44. Portable Electronic Music Synthesizer: the "Minimoog."

(Illustration courtesy of Moog Music, Inc.)

Unlike electronic organs with all their pre-fabricated sound imitations, chord progressions, and drum rhythms (see Fig. 33), the music synthesizer is the "compleat" do-it-yourself instrument. It generates its sounds electronically, but nothing is pre-set; the player creates all his own tone colors and noise signals and arranges for the desired "envelopes" (gradual or sharp attacks, and abrupt or fading sound-"decay"). The synthesizer permits "bending" of pitches and pitch-slides, it has filters with which to manipulate and modify sounds through highlighting or suppressing certain overtones and other sound-components, it can generate "white" and "pink" noise and all other unpitched clicks and hisses imaginable, and it can add signal-input from outside sources. (It also has earphones for silent practice.) A music synthesizer is the ideal instrument for experimentation with sound, but does not yet lend itself to traditional ways of performing music.

45. "The White House Steinway" as displayed in the East Room of the White House.

(Illustration courtesy of Steinway & Sons.)

This is the second White House Steinway. It was built in 1938 and bears the number 300,000.

Reference Biographical Dictionary
OF COMPOSERS REPRESENTED IN THE
New Scribner Music Library

COMPILED BY NICOLAS SLONIMSKY

AHRENDT, Karl, American composer. He was born in Toledo, Ohio, March 7, 1904. He studied violin and composition in Europe. Upon his return to America, he attended the Conservatory of Cincinnati (B.M., 1936). Later he received the degrees of M.M. (1937) and Ph.D. (1946) from the Eastman School of Music in Rochester. In 1950 he was appointed member of the faculty of the School of Music at Ohio University in Athens, Ohio. Among his compositions are many instrumental solos and ensembles, as well as choral pieces.

ALBÉNIZ, Isaac, celebrated national Spanish composer. He was born in Camprodón, May 29, 1860, and died in Cambo-les-Bains, France, May 18, 1909. He was an infant prodigy of the piano and played concerts in Paris and in Madrid, attracting considerable attention by the precocity of his musical gift. At the age of thirteen, he ran away from home, stowing away on a ship for Puerto Rico, then a Spanish possession. He subsequently travelled to Cuba and the United States where he played in saloons and vaudevilles. After his return to Europe in 1875, he undertook serious study at the Brussels Conservatory. Later he took lessons in composition with Jadassohn and Reinecke at the Leipzig Conservatory. In 1893 he settled in Paris. He wrote several operas, but they were not successful. His true vocation he found in piano music in the national Spanish vein. Of these pieces, his suite of twelve movements, *Iberia,* also makes use of impressionistic techniques in a virtuoso fashion. His smaller piano pieces, particularly *Tango,* attained great popularity.

ALT, Hansi, American pianist and composer. She was born in Vienna, February 25, 1911. She studied music at the University of Vienna. In 1941 she emigrated to the United States. After a few years of teaching piano at various schools, she opened a private studio in Washington. She published a number of piano pieces, distinguished by their fancifully descriptive manner. Their titles give a clue to their contents: *Parade, Sleepyhead, Splashing,* etc.

APPLEDORN, Mary Jeanne van, American composer. She was born in Holland, Michigan, October 2, 1927. She studied at the Eastman School of Music in Rochester, graduating in piano (B.M., 1948) and theory (M.M., 1950), and receiving her Ph.D. in composition there in 1966. She subsequently was chairman of the music department of Texas Technological University in Lubbock. Among her compositions are a piano concerto, *Burlesca* for piano, brass, and percussion, *Sonnet for Organ,* and a number of piano pieces in a Western style, among them *Apache Echoes, Boots 'n' Saddles, Café José, Indian Trail,* and *Wagon Train.*

ARENSKY, Anton, Russian composer. He was born in Novgorod, August 11, 1861, and died in Terijoki, Finland, February 25, 1906. He studied composition with Rimsky-Korsakov and later taught harmony and fugue at the Moscow Conservatory. Suffering from consumption, he spent his last years of life in Finnish health resorts. His music reflects the moods of Russian romanticism. Arensky was particularly successful in his piano works. His four suites for duo pianos are frequently performed.

ATTAIGNANT, Pierre, French musician of the Renaissance. He was born in the last decade of the fifteenth century and died in 1553. One of the earliest French music publishers to use movable type, he published a great many collections of dances and sacred works. He was also a composer of madrigals.

BACH, Carl Philipp Emanuel, known as the "Hamburg Bach," was the third son of Johann Sebastian Bach. He was born in Weimar, March 8, 1714, and died in Hamburg, December 14, 1788. He enrolled at the University of Leipzig as a student of philosophy and law and received his musical training at the hands of his father. In 1740 he was appointed chamber musician at the court of Frederick the Great. In 1767 he went to Hamburg where he succeeded Telemann as music director of principal Hamburg churches. He is regarded as the forerunner of the formal Classical school, departing from the great Bach's contrapuntal texture of composition. He wrote a fundamental instrumental manual, *Essay on the True Art of Playing Keyboard Instruments,* and composed several hundred instrumental pieces, as well as vocal works. His *Solfeggietto* in C minor for keyboard retains its popularity.

BACH, Johann Christian, eleventh and youngest surviving son of Johann Sebastian Bach, is also known as the "London Bach." He was born in Leipzig, September 5, 1735, and died in London, January 1, 1782. After the great Bach's death in 1750, he went to Berlin to study with his brother Carl Philipp Emanuel Bach and later with Padre Martini in Bologna. In 1762 he went to London where he was appointed music master to the Queen of England. Abandoning his father's contrapuntal style, he wrote instrumental pieces in a Rococo manner. He exercised decisive influence on Mozart's early development.

BACH, Johann Sebastian, the greatest composer of all time, whose very name, meaning "the stream," epitomizes his stature as the supreme source of inspiration.

He was born in Eisenach, March 21, 1685, and died in Leipzig, July 28, 1750. He learned the rudiments of music from his father, and the art of playing on keyboard instruments from his elder brother. Although to his contemporaries he appeared as a modest church organist, posterity soon discovered his greatness to be unequaled by any other musician of his time. Bach's works embrace the totality of music, except opera. It may be said, however, that his cantatas, Masses, and Passions possess a dramatic force surpassing that of most nominal operas. His two books of the *Well-tempered Clavier*, designed as a pedagogical work, have laid the foundation of the modulatory system of classical music. His last work, *The Art of the Fugue*, represents a landmark in contrapuntal ingenuity. The hypothesis of genetic inheritance of musical ability finds its corroboration in the genealogy of the Bach family, among his ancestors, lateral relatives, and his sons. Bach's second wife, Anna Magdalena, was herself a fine musician who often assisted Bach in filling out contrapuntal parts in his works. The *Notebook for Anna Magdalena Bach* was written for her a few years after their marriage which was blessed by thirteen children, several of whom became performers and composers in their own right.

BACH-GOUNOD. Gounod published *Méditation sur le premier Prélude de piano de S. Bach* for piano and violin solo with organ accompaniment in 1853. The words of the hymn *Ave Maria*, based on Archangel Gabriel's announcement to Mary, were added later. Gounod's arrangement became a perennial favorite with music lovers.

BACHMANN, Georges, pseudonym of Franz Behr who was born in Lübtheen, Mecklenburg, July 22, 1837, and died in Dresden, February 14, 1898. He wrote more than 3,000 piano pieces among which *Les Sylphes* (*Impromptu Valse*) has achieved popularity. Among Behr's other pseudonyms are William Cooper and Charles Morley.

BACON, Ernst, American composer. He was born in Chicago, May 26, 1898. He studied at the University of California, Berkeley, with Ernest Bloch. He won the Pulitzer Prize for music in 1932; also held a Guggenheim Fellowship. Apart from his compositions, Ernst Bacon distinguished himself as a writer and theorist. An erudite musician, he is nonetheless able to establish communication with music lovers of all strata. His piano pieces are invariably attractive while also dealing with specific technical problems. Among these charming little pieces are *Asleep in the Hay, The New-Laid Snow, The Rose Tree, Sparrows,* and *The White Church.*

BALFE, Michael William, Irish composer. He was born in Dublin, May 15, 1808, and died in Rowney Abbey, Hertfordshire, October 20, 1870. He studied violin and composition in Dublin, and later took courses in singing in Italy. He returned to London in 1835, and engaged himself in composing operas, of which *The Bohemian Girl* (1843) was extremely successful.

BANTOCK, Sir Granville, eminent English composer. He was born in London, August 7, 1868, and died there, October 16, 1946. He studied at the Royal Academy of Music, and began his career as a ballet composer. Possessing a cosmopolitan taste, he often used exotic subjects for his operas (*The Pearl of Iran*), ballets (*Egypt, The Great God Pan*), and symphonic poems (*The Witch of Atlas, Pagan Symphony, Omar Khayyám*). He also made effective arrangements of English folksongs, among them *Barbara Allen* and *Lord Rendal.*

BARLOW, Wayne, American organist and composer. He was born in Elyria, Ohio, September 6, 1912. He studied at the Eastman School of Music in Rochester, and in 1937 was appointed to its faculty. He also studied composition with Arnold Schoenberg in Los Angeles. He held two Fulbright Grants, one for Denmark in 1955, and one for Belgium and Holland in 1964. He published a treatise on music appreciation, *Foundations of Music,* and various teaching pieces.

BARNARD, Charlotte Alington (Claribel), English composer. She was born in London, December 23, 1830, and died in Dover, January 30, 1869. In 1866, under the pen name Claribel, she published a song, *Come Back to Erin,* to her own words, which became popular. It is interesting to note that although the words and music of this song reflect the Irish sentiment, their author was English.

BARNBY, Sir Joseph, English organist and composer. He was born in York, August 12, 1838, and died in London, January 28, 1896. He was a chorister at the York Minster, studied at the Royal Academy in London, and held various posts as organist in London. In 1864 he formed Barnby's Choir with which he performed oratorios and other sacred works. He was knighted in 1892. His setting of Tennyson's poem *Sweet and Low,* composed in 1863, became a favorite in England and America.

BARTÓK, Béla, great Hungarian composer who exercised decisive influence on the evolution of modern music. He was born in Nagy Szent-Miklós, Transylvania, March 25, 1881, and died in New York, September 26, 1945. He studied at the Royal Academy of Music in Budapest, where he later became an instructor. An excellent pianist, he confined his programs mostly to his own music. In his later years he played duo piano with his second wife, Ditta Pasztory. In 1927–1928 Bartók made his first American tour, playing recitals of his own music. The critical reception was adverse, for Bartók's style, marked by angular rhythms and aggressive dissonances, was repugnant to the majority of American concert-goers. Bartók returned to Europe, living mostly in Budapest as teacher and composer. After the outbreak of World War II, he again made his way to the United States, where he remained until his death due to leukemia. In his music, Bartók did not pursue modernism for modernism's sake; in spite of a host of innovative techniques, he remained faithful to basic tonality. Most of his compositions are permeated with the spirit of Hungarian folk rhythms. Under the title *Mikrokosmos,* he published a remarkable collection of 153 progressive pieces for piano, designed to educate beginners in modern techniques; he also made numerous arrangements of Hungarian, Rumanian, and Slavic folksongs.

BEACH, Mrs. H. H. A. (Amy Marcy Cheney), American composer. She was born in Henniker, New Hampshire, September 5, 1867, and died in New York, December 27, 1944. At the age of eighteen she married Dr. H. H. A. Beach of Boston. She had no regular instruction in composition, but acquired an impressive technique by studying classical and romantic works. Her *Gallic Symphony* (1896) was the first full-fledged symphonic work by an American woman. In 1900 she played her piano concerto with the Boston Symphony Orchestra. She also composed chamber music, songs, and piano music, all written in an unaffected, pleasing manner.

BECK, Martha, American composer. Born in Sodaville, Oregon, January 19, 1900, she was educated at Oberlin Conservatory (B.M., 1924) and at the American Conservatory in Chicago (M.M., 1929). After her marriage to G. Howard Carragan she settled in Troy, New York, as a piano teacher. Many of her piano pieces are inspired by exotic subjects, such as *Chinese Holiday, East Indian Pony Express,* and *In Old Japan.* She also wrote chamber music and choruses.

BECKHELM, Paul, American composer. He was born in Kankakee, Illinois, July 3, 1906, and died in Mt. Vernon, Iowa, November 6, 1966. He studied at Northwestern University (B.M., 1927), Fort Hays, Kansas, State College (B.S., 1930), and at the Eastman School of Music in Rochester (M.M., 1938; Ph.D., 1949). He wrote many works for various instrumental groups and composed successful teaching pieces for piano, among them *Carefree Days, Hobgoblins, Melancholy, Sidewalk Games, Sunday Bells,* and *Toppling Over.*

BEESON, Jack, American pianist and composer. He was born in Muncie, Indiana, July 15, 1921. He studied with Howard Hanson and Bernard Rogers at the Eastman School of Music in Rochester, where he obtained his Ph.D. He also took private lessons with Béla Bartók during the latter's stay in New York. He was a member of the faculty of the Juilliard School of Music and later joined the staff of Columbia University where, in 1966, he became the head of the music department. His opera *Lizzie Borden,* produced in New York in 1965, was well received. He also wrote a television opera, *My Heart's in the Highlands* (1970), a symphony, five piano sonatas, and some effective teaching pieces for piano.

BEETHOVEN, Ludwig van, supreme master of music, great equally in symphonic, vocal, chamber music, and instrumental solo works. He was born in Bonn, December 16, 1770, and died in Vienna, March 26, 1827. The Beethoven family was of Flemish extraction, which explains the appended nobiliary particle "van." Beethoven played the violin as well as the piano as a child, and held a salaried position as an assistant organist at the age of fourteen. In 1792 he moved to Vienna where he had lessons with Haydn. When he was about thirty years old, his deafness, the origin of which is obscure, began to afflict him seriously. He virtually abandoned his career as an artist and performer and dedicated himself entirely to composition. His greatest works relate to his Vienna period, comprising the *Eroica Symphony* (No. 3), the *Pastoral Symphony* (No. 6), the violin concerto, the piano concertos, thirty-two piano sonatas (including the *Moonlight Sonata* and the *Sonata Appassionata*), violin sonatas, cello sonatas, trios, and string quartets, culminating in the sublime *Ninth Symphony* with its choral finale. His only opera, *Fidelio,* and his *Missa Solemnis* testify to Beethoven's power in vocal writing. Beethoven's personal life was unhappy; ever increasing deafness cast an almost impenetrable curtain of silence on his world and gave him a sense of social separation despite numerous admirers and faithful disciples. An uncouth genius, he lacked mundane graces. Possessed with passionate feelings of love, he never married or had a liaison. His famous letter to "the immortal beloved," apparently the product of a platonic fantasy, was never dispatched to the hypothetical lady of his dreams.

BERG, Alban, remarkable Austrian composer. He was born in Vienna, February 9, 1885, and died there, December 24, 1935. A meeting with Arnold Schoenberg determined his direction in composition: he became Schoenberg's ardent disciple and adopted wholeheartedly the method of composing with twelve tones related only to one another, known as the dodecaphonic system. However, the exclusion of tonality and the avoidance of all triadic connotations, essential to Schoenberg's own style of composition, was not binding to Berg who freely expanded the method to include harmonious combinations. It may be said that Berg humanized Schoenberg's austere art without undermining its fundamentals. Berg's opera *Wozzeck* was produced in Berlin on December 14, 1925. Its uncompromisingly dissonant idiom and unconventional operatic structure evoked violent criticism but in time the opera achieved the status of a modern classic. His second opera, *Lulu,* written in the twelve-tone technique, remained uncompleted. Berg's last work was a violin concerto which by now has become a regular part of the modern virtuoso repertory.

BERLIOZ, Hector, great French composer whose music inaugurated the Romantic era. He was born in Côte-Saint-André, December 11, 1803, and died in Paris, March 8, 1869. He studied medicine before turning to music. He entered the Paris Conservatory as a student of Lesueur and Reicha, obtaining the second Prix de Rome in 1828 and the first Prix de Rome in 1830. He was twenty-six when he composed his historic masterpiece *Symphonie Fantastique,* breaking away from classical form and replacing individual themes by a unifying "idée fixe." His concert opera *The Damnation of Faust* contains the famous *Rákóczi March,* the *Minuet of the Will-o'-the-Wisps,* and *Dance of the Sylphs.* His dramatic symphony *Romeo and Juliet* is another significant work, and so is his monumental *Requiem Mass.* Berlioz also wrote several song cycles of which *Les Nuits d'Été* is notable.

BERNARDONE, Anka (pen name of Sister Mary Ann Joyce), American pianist and composer. She was born in Champaign, Illinois, October 3, 1937. She attended Washington University and Fontbonne College in St. Louis. Her principal piano teacher was Sister John Joseph Bezdek. She also studied the interpretation of Bach with Rosalyn Turek. She holds a Ph.D. in composition from Washington University and is on the faculty at Fontbonne College. Her works include choruses and a number of teaching pieces for piano, among them *Dance of the Clocks, Lullaby for a Faun, Parade in the Glen,* and *The Winding River.*

BEZDEK, Jan (pseudonym of Sister John Joseph Bezdek), American pianist and composer. She was born in St. Louis, Missouri, August 29, 1896. She studied piano with Rudolf Ganz and composition with Felix Borowski at the Chicago Musical College, and later took courses at the Eastman School of Music in Rochester, receiving her Ph.D. there in 1946. In 1972 she was professor emerita at Fontbonne College in St. Louis. Under the pseudonym Jan Bezdek, she published some characteristic piano pieces, among them *Bells, Holding On, The Little Bird,* and *Marching.* Under another pseudonym, Julia Derleth, she published *A Bird is Singing, The Fiddler's Tune,* and *Waltz in G Minor* for piano. She was a member of the editorial board of the Scribner Music Library.

BISHOP, Sir Henry Rowley, English composer. He was born in London, November 18, 1786, and died there, April 30, 1855. Connected with the theater practically all of his life, he wrote a great number of operas, vaudevilles, ballets, and ballads, but he owes his fame entirely to the song *Home, Sweet Home* (set to the text of the American poet John Howard Payne), which appears in his opera *Clari,* produced in London in 1823.

BIZET, Georges, great French opera composer. He was born in Paris, October 25, 1838, and died at Bougival, June 3, 1875. He entered the Paris Conservatory at the age of nine and studied composition with Halévy whose daughter he later married. He received the Grand Prix de Rome in 1857. His symphonic suite *L'Arlésienne* became a perennial favorite, but it was his opera *Carmen,* produced at the Opéra-Comique in Paris on March 3, 1875, that made Bizet's name immortal. A realistic libretto, centered on a Spanish cigarette girl who ruins the life of an infatuated soldier only to abandon him for a bullfighter, provided a dramatic story which Bizet was able to convert into a marvellously melodious score. In the French libretto, the bullfighter is called Toreador, but the proper Spanish word is Torero. The famous *Habanera* is not by Bizet; he borrowed it from a collection of Spanish songs by Sebastián Yradier.

BLON, Franz von, German composer. He was born in Berlin, July 16, 1861, and died in Seilershof, October 21, 1945. He was active as a theater-orchestra conductor in Berlin and Hamburg, and wrote several operettas, overtures, waltzes, and a great number of marches.

BLOW, John, great English composer and organist. He was born in Newark-on-Trent in February, 1649, and died in London, October 1, 1708. He was appointed organist at Westminster Abbey at the age of nineteen, and held the post until his death, with a hiatus of several years when his student, the famous composer Purcell, was organist. John Blow wrote a great number of sacred choral and vocal works, and also instrumental music in the polyphonic style.

BOCCHERINI, Luigi, famous Italian composer. He was born in Lucca, February 19, 1743, and died in Madrid, Spain, May 28, 1805. He studied in Rome, then moved to Paris. After the French Revolution, he settled in Madrid as a chamber composer at the Spanish court. Boccherini wrote a great deal of instrumental music. His stylistic affinity to Haydn gave cause to the facetious phrase "Boccherini is the wife of Haydn." Boccherini's most famous separate number is his *Minuet,* extracted from his string quintet of 1771.

BOHN, Carl, German pianist. He was born in Berlin, September 11, 1844, and died there, April 4, 1920. He studied and lived most of his life in Berlin. His piano pieces enjoyed considerable popularity. Of these, *La Zingara,* a Hungarian gypsy dance, is notable.

BOREL-CLERC, Charles, French composer of popular music. He was born in Pau, September 22, 1879, and died in Cannes, April 9, 1959. In 1903 he composed *La Mattchiche* which became a universal hit. In the United States it was published under the title *La Sorella.* A children's rhyme was adapted to the tune: "My Ma gave me a nickel, to buy a pickle; I didn't buy a pickle, I bought some chewing gum."

BORODIN, Alexander, Russian composer. He was born in St. Petersburg, November 12, 1833, and died there, February 27, 1887. He studied chemistry and contributed learned research papers on scientific subjects; music was his avocation. Borodin is known to history as a member of the "Mighty Five," a group that included Balakirev, Cui, Mussorgsky, and Rimsky-Korsakov. Because of the pressure of his academic preoccupations, Borodin did not finish his greatest work, the opera *Prince Igor,* which was completed after Borodin's death by Rimsky-Korsakov and Glazunov. He also wrote two symphonies, a symphonic tableau *In Central Asia,* chamber music, and songs. Among his piano pieces, his *Little Suite* is a popular concert number.

BOROWSKI, Felix, American composer and critic. He was born in Burton, England, March 10, 1872, and died in Chicago, September 6, 1956. After study in London and in Germany, he emigrated in 1897 to the United States, taught at the Chicago Musical College and at Northwestern University, wrote music criticism, and served as program annotator for the Chicago Symphony Orchestra. He composed several attractive violin and piano pieces which became popular.

BOURGEOIS, Louis, French composer of religious music. He was born in Paris about 1510 and died there about 1561. A disciple of Calvin, he adapted hymn tunes for Calvinist services.

BRAHMS, Johannes, great master of German music. He was born in Hamburg, May 7, 1833, and died in Vienna, April 3, 1897. He studied rudiments of music with his father, a double-bass player. Later he took lessons in piano. Hans von Bülow described Brahms as the "Third B of Music" after Bach and Beethoven, and the phrase became popular. Indeed, Brahms occupies a historic position within both the Classical and Romantic Schools. Contrary to Romantic practices, his four symphonies contain no programmatic allusions; similarly, Brahms preferred to use formal rather than descriptive titles for his instrumental music. As composer of German Lieder, however, Brahms was a true successor of the Romanticists Schubert and Schumann. Brahms often appeared as soloist in his two piano concertos and as conductor of his symphonies and overtures. In 1878 he moved to Vienna where he remained until his death.

BRITTEN, Benjamin, the most significant British composer of the twentieth century. He was born in Lowestoft, Suffolk, November 22, 1913. He studied composition with Frank Bridge, then entered the Royal College of Music where his teachers were John Ireland in composition and Arthur Benjamin in piano. Britten began to compose very early in life. His works, set in a decisively modern manner, possess a singular power of communication. He is particularly successful in his operas of which *Peter Grimes* achieved the status of a modern classic; an instrumental interlude from it, *Dawn*, with its striking imitations of seagull cries, is often performed in concert form. Britten wrote a remarkably apt orchestral set, *The Young Person's Guide to the Orchestra*, illustrating the use of individual instruments.

BULL, John, English madrigalist. He was born in Somersetshire, England, about 1562, and died in Antwerp, March 12, 1628. As a young man, he played the organ at the Chapel Royal. In 1613 he went to Brussels as an organist, and in 1617 he became organist at the Cathedral of Notre Dame at Antwerp. John Bull composed some two hundred pieces of contrapuntal keyboard music and many ballads in the popular style of his time.

BUXTEHUDE, Dietrich, one of the great masters of contrapuntal music before Bach. He was born in Denmark about 1637, but his exact birth place has not been established. Three municipalities vie for the honor— Elsinore, Hälsingborg, and Oldesloe. All belonged to Denmark at the time of his birth, though only one still does today. He died in Lübeck, Germany, May 9, 1707. In 1668 he succeeded the famous organist Franz Tunder at the church of St. Mary in Lübeck, and in 1673 he inaugurated the renowned Evening Concerts (*Abendmusiken*) with programs of organ and choral music. Handel travelled to hear Buxtehude play in 1703, and so did Bach in 1705, both in the hope of obtaining the Lübeck post after the master's retirement. However, both were deterred from their applications by the notorious marriage clause, requiring the successor to marry the incumbent's daughter, Buxtehude's five daughters being exceedingly ugly. Buxtehude's stylistic influence on both Handel and Bach was substantial and is manifested particularly in Bach's organ chorale preludes and his *Passacaglia*.

CAMPBELL, Aline (pen name of Merle Montgomery), American pianist, composer, and editor. She was born in Davidson, Oklahoma, May 15, 1904. She studied at the University of Oklahoma, receiving her B.F.A. there in 1924. She then enrolled at the Eastman School of Music, Rochester, where she obtained her Ph.D. She also studied piano with Isidor Philipp in Paris and took a course in composition with Nadia Boulanger at the American Conservatory in Fontainebleau. She subsequently occupied teaching posts at the University of Oklahoma and at the Eastman School of Music. She served as advisor to several music publishing firms, and was active as a lecturer. She published some valuable music manuals for schools, and piano pieces of a descriptive nature, such as *A Camel Ride*. (*For additional biographical information see Volume 1.*)

CAMPION, Thomas, English poet, composer, and playwright. He was born in London, February 12, 1567, and died there, March 1, 1620. His historical significance rests in his many songs, for which he wrote his own texts.

CAMPRA, André, French opera composer. He was born in Aix-en-Provence, December 4, 1660, and died in Versailles, June 29, 1744. He occupied posts as organist and music director in French cathedrals, culminating in his appointment at Notre Dame in Paris. He produced a number of operas on mythological subjects and published several cycles of songs and dances.

CAREY, Henry, English poet and composer. He was born in Yorkshire, about 1687, and died (committed suicide) in London, October 4, 1743. He studied music with Geminiani in London where he settled in 1710. Carey was a facile composer of popular songs, but his chief claim to fame is the putative authorship of the tune of *God Save the King*. The tune is also used for the American anthem *My Country 'tis of Thee*, the words for which were written by the Boston clergyman Samuel Francis Smith.

CARPENTER, John Alden, American composer. He was born in Park Ridge, Illinois, February 28, 1876, and died in Chicago, April 26, 1951. He studied music at Harvard University with John K. Paine. After graduation, he joined his father's shipping supply firm. However, he continued to pursue his musical studies and eventually earned for himself a significant place in American music, mainly because of his experimental works on American subjects, of which *Skyscrapers*, a ballet, was notable. He also wrote symphonic works, chamber music, and songs.

CHABRIER, Emmanuel, French composer. He was born in Ambert, January 18, 1841, and died in Paris, September 13, 1894. He studied law and piano; subsequently took lessons with Duparc and Vincent d'Indy. He was a member of the French group of composers seeking to promulgate Wagner's ideas of music drama. He wrote operas, but achieved fame by his Spanish-flavored instrumental pieces, especially *España* for orchestra and *Habanera* for piano.

CHAMINADE, Cécile, French composer of light pieces, mostly for piano. She was born in Paris, August 8, 1857, and died in Monte Carlo, April 18, 1944. She studied composition with Benjamin Godard. Several of her piano pieces, possessing an unaffected charm, particularly *Scarf Dance*, attained great popularity among music lovers.

CHOPIN, Frédéric, great Polish composer who revolutionized the art of writing for the piano. He was born in Zelazowa Wola, near Warsaw, March 1, 1810, and died in Paris, October 17, 1849. His father was a teacher of French, who emigrated to Poland and married a Polish woman. Chopin studied in Warsaw with Joseph Elsner, and made appearances as a child pianist. After a series of concerts in Germany and Austria, he went to Paris in 1831 and remained there. He formed friendships with Liszt, Berlioz, and other artists in Paris. The critics bestowed upon him the Shakespearian description "the Ariel of the piano," alluding to the poetic quality of his playing. Chopin was afflicted with tuberculosis and died before reaching the age of forty. His role in creating a new type of virtuoso piano technique is immeasurable; he converted the piano, technically a percussion instrument, to a medium of melodious song supported by now delicate, now powerful harmonic sonorities. He wrote two piano concertos, sonatas, etudes, nocturnes, waltzes, scherzos, polonaises, preludes, impromptus, and ballades. While reputations of many other Romantic composers have dimmed, Chopin's music retains its magical appeal for generation after generation of musicians and music lovers.

CLARIBEL. See BARNARD, Charlotte Alington.

CLARK, Elizabeth Mary, American pianist and composer. She was born in Placerville, California, June 5, 1917. She studied in Stockton, California, and later at the Eastman School of Music in Rochester. She was married to the composer Bernard Rogers. Her compositions include two piano concertos, song cycles, chamber music, and a number of teaching pieces, among them *Cradle Song*, *Oriental Song*, and *The Rocking Chair*.

CLEMENTI, Muzio, celebrated Italian composer and educator. He was born in Rome, January 23, 1752, and died in Evesham, England, March 10, 1832. He studied organ and piano in Italy and was taken to London by a rich English philanthropist. Later he embarked on a European tour as pianist. Returning to London, he founded a piano factory and a publishing house. His masterwork is a book of piano studies, *Gradus ad Parnassum* (1817), which became a classic of pedagogical literature. The Latin title means Steps (in plural) to Mt. Parnassus, the mountain sacred to the Muses.

COHAN, George M., American composer whose song *Over There* became a patriotic classic of the American Expeditionary Force in World War I. He was born in Providence, Rhode Island, July 3, 1878, and died in New York, November 5, 1942. He appeared as a singer in vaudeville and composed popular ballads. He received a congressional medal for his contributions, and a monument was erected to him in New York City.

COPLAND, Aaron, one of the most significant American composers of the twentieth century. He was born in Brooklyn, November 14, 1900. He studied piano with Victor Wittgenstein and Clarence Adler, and theory with Rubin Goldmark. In 1921 he went to Paris where he took courses in composition and orchestration with Nadia Boulanger. He enjoyed early support of Serge Koussevitzky, then conductor of the Boston Symphony Orchestra with which he appeared as soloist in his piano concerto in 1927, producing a *succès de scandale* with staid Boston audiences and critics. His *Lincoln Portrait* for speaker and orchestra and the ballets *Billy the Kid, Rodeo,* and *Appalachian Spring* became modern American classics. He also wrote works of a purely abstract nature, among them *Connotations* for orchestra, commissioned for the inauguration of Lincoln Center in New York in 1962. He received many honors, including the Medal of Freedom bestowed upon him by the U.S. Government, honorary doctorates, the Pulitzer Prize, the New York Music Critics Award, etc. His film score for *The Heiress* won an Academy Award. Copland appeared often as guest conductor with major symphony orchestras in Europe and America. He also was guest lecturer at Harvard and other universities. He was head of the composition department of the Berkshire Music Center at Tanglewood from 1940 to 1965. His vocal cycle *Twelve Poems of Emily Dickinson* (1950) is an innovative work of American art song.

COUPERIN, François, great French composer and organist, surnamed Le Grand. He was born in Paris, November 10, 1668, and died there, September 12, 1733. He became organist of St. Gervais in Paris at the age of seventeen and held this position until his death. He enjoyed the favor of Louis XIV, for whom he composed music to be played at court. His suites for keyboard instruments are ingenious in form, melody, and rhythm; some movements are descriptive of moods and scenes. He also published a manual, *L'Art de toucher le Clavecin* (1716).

COUPERIN, Louis, founding member of the great French family of organists and keyboard composers. He was born in Chaumes in 1626 and died in Paris, August 29, 1661. He became organist of St. Gervais, where François Couperin, who was his nephew, was later employed. Louis Couperin wrote a number of dances for the keyboard, usually grouped in suites. His gigue *Canarie* (a rapid French dance supposedly imitating the primitive rhythms of the aborigines of the Canary Islands) is popular.

CRESTON, Paul, American composer of the modern school. His real name was Joseph Guttoveggio. He was born in New York, of Italian parents, October 10, 1906.

He studied piano with G. Aldo Randegger and Gaston Déthier and organ with Pietro Yon. In composition, he was entirely self-taught. He held two Guggenheim Fellowships. At various times, he was president of the National Association of American Composers and Conductors and a member of the executive committee of the National Music Council. In 1960 he travelled to Israel and Turkey as a music specialist. A highly productive composer, he wrote five symphonies, numerous other symphonic works, a saxophone concerto, an accordion concerto, two violin concertos, a concertino for marimba and orchestra, a piano concerto, a concerto for two pianos, and many pieces of chamber music in various combinations. He also published a book, *Principles of Rhythm* (New York, 1964).

CRIST, Bainbridge, American composer. He was born in Lawrenceburg, Indiana, February 13, 1883, and died in Barnstable, Massachusetts, February 7, 1969. He studied music and law, received his L.L.B. at George Washington University, and practiced law in Boston from 1906 to 1912. He then went to Europe where he studied singing with William Shakespeare in London and composition with Paul Juon in Berlin. Returning to America, he taught singing and wrote music as an avocation. His compositions are set in an attractive, romantic manner. Some of them are of exotic inspiration, such as *Icelandic Cradle Song*, others are couched in simple dance rhythms (*Jig, A Country Dance,* etc.).

CROFT, William, English organist and composer. He was born in Nether Ettington, Warwickshire, December 30, 1678, and died in Bath, August 14, 1727. He was a chorister in the Chapel Royal, where he became organist in 1707, and succeeded Dr. John Blow as organist of Westminster Abbey in 1708. Croft was a prolific composer of anthems and ballads.

CROUCH, Frederick Nicholls, English song composer. He was born in London, July 31, 1808, and died in Portland, Maine, August 18, 1896. He studied at the Royal Academy of Music, and was at various times a singer and a cellist in London theaters. In 1856 he emigrated to the United States. He joined the Confederate Army during the Civil War, then taught singing in Baltimore. His song *Kathleen Mavourneen* became a perennial favorite. (His daughter attained a high social status as a Parisian courtesan during the Second Empire under the name of Cora Pearl.)

CUI, César, Russian composer, one of the group of the "Mighty Five." He was born in Vilna, Lithuania, January 18, 1835, and died in Petrograd, March 26, 1918. His father was a French soldier in Napoleon's Army, who remained in Russia; his mother was Lithuanian. Cui studied military engineering in St. Petersburg and became a specialist in fortification. He was at one time tutor to Czar Nicholas II, when the latter was heir to the throne. In music, he was mainly self-taught. Although a nationalist, Cui wrote music of a delicate, romantic nature. His poetic miniature *Orientale,* available in numerous arrangements, is a perennial favorite.

CUTLER, Henry Stephen, American organist and hymn composer. He was born in Boston, October 13, 1824, and died there, December 5, 1902. He studied organ in Germany. Returning to America, he occupied various posts as church organist in Boston, New York, Providence, and Philadelphia. Of his anthems, *The Son of God Goes Forth to War* is the best known.

CZIBULKA, Alphons, Hungarian musician. He was born in Szepes-Várallya, May 14, 1842, and died in Vienna, October 27, 1894. He was employed as military bandmaster in Vienna and Prague. Some ballet numbers from his operas retain their popularity.

DANDRIEU, Jean François, French composer. He was born about 1682 and died in Paris, January 16, 1738. He served as an organist in Paris and published a number of keyboard pieces, some of them bearing descriptive titles although remaining strictly classical in form.

DAQUIN, Louis-Claude, French organist and composer. He was born in Paris, July 4, 1694, and died there, June 15, 1772. He played the organ at various Paris churches as a child. In 1739 he was appointed organist at St. Paul in Paris after winning a competition with Rameau. He published several collections of keyboard pieces; of these, *Le Coucou* has become a great favorite. It is based on a falling minor third, imitating the familiar call of the cuckoo.

DEBUSSY, Claude, great French composer, creator of the new musical language of 'Impressionism.' He was born in St. Germaine-en-Laye, August 22, 1862, and died in Paris, March 25, 1918. Because of his precocious gifts, he was admitted to the Paris Conservatory at the age of eleven, where he studied piano with Marmontel and composition with Durand. In 1880 he was engaged by Mme. Nadezhda von Meck, Tchaikovsky's benefactress, as a piano tutor in Moscow where he became acquainted with Russian music which exercised some influence on his own development as a composer. Returning to Paris, he continued his studies at the Conservatory, and in 1884 he was awarded the Grand Prix de Rome for his cantata *L'Enfant prodigue.* After a mandatory stay in Rome, he travelled in Germany. His early enthusiasm for Wagner was soon dispelled by emotional antagonism, partly on patriotic grounds. In Paris he joined the circle of French symbolist poets and impressionist painters and evolved a unique style of composition, marked by an extreme delicacy of expression, exotic flavor, and a free use of unresolved dissonances. His piano suite *Bergamasque* (1890) is an early example of his new, Impressionist style of composition; it includes the celebrated piece *Clair de lune.* With his orchestral *Prélude à l'après-midi d'un faune* (1894), Debussy achieved a high degree of the expressive use of tone color. It was followed by his symphonic tableau *La Mer.* The quintessence of Debussy's vocal style is exemplified by his opera *Pelléas et*

Mélisande, produced at the Opéra-Comique in Paris on April 30, 1902, which remains one of the greatest masterpieces of operatic art of the twentieth century.

DE KOVEN, Reginald, American composer. He was born in Middletown, Connecticut, April 3, 1859, and died in Chicago, January 16, 1920. He studied piano and composition in Germany and in France. Returning to America, he was active as a conductor and operetta composer. His fame derives from the celebrated song *Oh, Promise Me!* which was first published separately in 1889 and was subsequently introduced into De Koven's operetta *Robin Hood* at its Chicago performance in 1890.

DELIBES, Léo, famous French composer for the theater. He was born in St.-Germain-du-Val, Sarthe, February 21, 1836, and died in Paris, January 16, 1891. He studied at the Paris Conservatory and later was organist at Paris churches. After an indifferent success of his operettas, he turned to the composition of ballet scores, revealing himself as a master of the genre. His ballets *Coppélia* (1870) and *Sylvia* (1876) became famous. In 1883 he produced his operatic masterpiece *Lakmé*. His melodic facility and rhythmic felicity won for him an honorable place in the annals of theatrical music. His incidental music for Victor Hugo's play *Le Roi s'amuse* also enjoyed popularity.

DENZA, Luigi, Italian song composer. He was born in Castellammare di Stabia, February 24, 1846, and died in London, January 26, 1922. He studied at the Naples Conservatory and in 1879 settled in London as a singing teacher. He was the composer of the famous Neapolitan ballad *Funiculi, Funicula,* which is often mistaken for a genuine folksong.

DERLETH, Julia, pseudonym for Sister John Joseph Bezdek. (*see* BEZDEK, Jan).

DESTOUCHES, André-Cardinal, French opera composer. He was born in Paris, April 6, 1672, and died there, February 3, 1749. He went to Siam as a missionary. Returning to France in 1688, he wrote pastoral operas. A *Canarie* (a French dance, supposed to imitate the primitive rhythms of the aborigines of the Canary Islands) from his opera *Amadis de Grèce* became popular.

DIABELLI, Anton, Austrian composer and publisher. He was born in Mattsee, near Salzburg, September 5, 1781, and died in Vienna, April 8, 1858. He settled in Vienna as a teacher. In 1818 he joined a publishing company. Diabelli's name remains in the annals of music owing to the fact that Beethoven wrote a set of thirty-three variations on a waltz tune by him.

DIAMOND, David, American composer. He was born in Rochester, New York, July 9, 1915. He attended the Cleveland Institute and later studied composition with Bernard Rogers at the Eastman School of Music in Rochester, Roger Sessions in New York, and Nadia Boulanger in Paris. He held three Guggenheim Fellowships. For a number of years he lived in Florence, Italy. Diamond composed eight symphonies, much chamber music, and vocal works. His piano music includes a concerto for piano and orchestra, a concerto for two pianos and orchestra, a sonata, and a set of piano pieces, *Album for the Young.* While most of his major compositions employ complex techniques, he knows how to write in a simple manner for non-professionals and music lovers.

DI CAPUA, Eduardo, Italian composer of Neapolitan ballads. He was born in Naples in 1864 and died there in 1917. He owes his fame to his song '*O Sole Mio!,* which became a favorite all over the world. Another famous song written by him was *Maria, Marì.* He sold these songs to a publisher for a pittance and died in poverty.

DIEMER, Emma Lou, American composer and educator. She was born in Kansas City, Missouri, November 24, 1927. She attended Yale University and the Eastman School of Music in Rochester, where she obtained her Ph.D. in composition. Her works include *Youth Overture* for orchestra, *Pavane* for string orchestra, chamber music, choruses, and instrumental solos.

DITTERSDORF, Karl von, Austrian violinist and composer. He was born in Vienna, November 2, 1739, and died at Castle Rothlhotta, near Neuhof, Bohemia, October 24, 1799. He was active as concertmaster and conductor at the Court Theater in Vienna, and later was attached to various princely houses in Silesia. He wrote many operas marked by expertise and considerable melodic invention.

DOHNÁNYI, Ernst von, eminent Hungarian pianist and composer of the Romantic School. He was born in Pressburg, July 27, 1877, and died in New York, February 9, 1960. He studied at the Budapest Academy of Music. After graduation he took lessons in composition with Eugen d'Albert. Dohnányi had a successful career as a concert pianist. He taught piano in Berlin and in Budapest, and also conducted the Budapest Philharmonic Orchestra. He remained in Hungary during World War II, but settled in the United States in 1949 as professor of piano and composition at Florida State College in Tallahassee. His music is distinguished by its mastery of form and technique, particularly in his piano works which continue to enjoy performances.

DOWLAND, John, famous lute player and composer. He was born in Ireland in 1562 and died in London, January 21, 1626. He went to London as a young boy and subsequently travelled in France, Germany, and Italy. For a time he was court lutenist to the King of Denmark, Christian IV, returning to England in 1609. His songs and dances enjoyed great renown for their contrapuntal excellence. Several books containing his instrumental and vocal works were published during his lifetime.

DRDLA, Franz, Bohemian violinist and composer. He was born in Saar, Moravia, November 28, 1868, and died in Gastein, September 3, 1944. He studied violin at the Vienna Conservatory and for many years was a member of the orchestra of the Vienna Court Opera. From 1923 to 1925 he lived in the U.S.; then returned to Europe.

His fame rests on his melodious violin solo, *Souvenir*, which became a perennial favorite.

DRIGO, Riccardo, Italian composer of theatrical music. He was born in Padua, June 30, 1846, and died there, October 1, 1930. Invited to Russia, he became conductor at the Imperial Opera in St. Petersburg, in 1879. The *Serenade* from his ballet *Arlequin's Millions* (1900) is famous. Also popular is his *Valse Bluette.*

DURAND, Marie-Auguste, French composer and publisher. He was born in Paris, July 18, 1830, and died there, May 31, 1909. He served as organist at several Paris churches; in 1870 he founded the famous French publishing firm which eventually became known as A. Durand & Fils. As a composer, Durand contributed a number of pleasing piano pieces of which *Valse brillante* has become greatly popular.

DUSSEK, Jan Ladislav, important Czech composer. He was born in Cáslav, Bohemia, February 12, 1760, and died in St.-Germain-en-Laye, March 20, 1812. He occupied various posts as organist in Bohemia and in the Netherlands, studied briefly with Carl Philipp Emanuel Bach in Hamburg in 1783, and was subsequently in the service of several courts in Germany and Austria. Apart from his virtuosity as a keyboard performer, Dussek wrote an immense number of piano works in various combinations with other instruments. His piano sonatas and sonatinas still retain their popularity with pianists.

DVOŘÁK, Antonín, great Bohemian composer. He was born in Mühlhausen, September 8, 1841, and died in Prague, May 1, 1904. He studied violin and played in the orchestra of the National Theater in Prague, but began to compose relatively late in life. Encouraged by Brahms, Dvořák embarked on the composition of large symphonic and choral works and operas. In 1892 he was engaged as the artistic director of the National Conservatory in New York, a post that he kept until 1895. His most famous symphony, entitled *From the New World,* was composed in America and first performed by the New York Philharmonic on December 15, 1893. He also wrote the celebrated piano solo *Humoresque* in America. A very prolific composer, Dvořák produced a great number of pieces of chamber music, concertos, and vocal works, both sacred and secular. Several of his early symphonies were not published until many years after his death, which created a certain confusion in their numbering. Thus the *New World Symphony,* formerly listed as No. 5, is now catalogued as No. 9.

DVORKIN, Judith, American pianist and composer. She was born in New York in 1930, and attended Barnard College and Columbia University where she studied composition with Otto Luening. Her other teachers were Elliott Carter and Roger Sessions. Her published works consist chiefly of songs, piano solos, and choruses. She also wrote some orchestral and chamber music. Her one-act opera *Crescent Eyebrow* was performed in New York in 1956.

DYKES, John Bacchus, English writer of hymn tunes. He was born at Kingston-upon-Hull, March 10, 1823, and died at Ticehurst, Sussex, January 22, 1876. He played the organ in his grandfather's church as a child, then entered Cambridge University, graduating in 1847. Later he served as canon, precentor, and vicar in Durham. His numerous anthems, written in a polyphonic style, became popular in English and American churches.

ELGAR, Edward, one of the most important composers of the modern English national school. He was born in Broadheath, near Worcester, June 2, 1857, and died in Worcester, February 23, 1934. His father was an organist at St. George's Roman Catholic Church in Worcester, and Elgar received his musical training from him. In 1879 he was appointed bandmaster at the County Lunatic Asylum in Worcester, and in 1885 he assumed his father's post as organist at St. George's. Elgar made his mark as a composer in 1899 with the brilliant and ingenious orchestral *Variations on an Original Theme,* generally known as *Enigma Variations;* its fourteen sections are identified by initials or nicknames of his friends. His impressive oratorio *The Dream of Gerontius* followed in 1900. But the most popular of Elgar's works proved to be the first of a group of marches under the title *Pomp and Circumstance.* The tune of the first march was later set to words, *Land of Hope and Glory,* and became a semi-official patriotic British anthem. It has also been adopted in American schools as a valedictory march at commencement exercises. Elgar's early piece *Salut d'Amour* (1889), originally written for orchestra, was later arranged by him for violin and piano and for piano solo.

ELVEY, George J., English organist and composer. He was born in Canterbury, March 27, 1816, and died at Windlesham, Surrey, December 9, 1893. He studied at the Royal Academy of Music, then served as organist at St. George's Chapel, Windsor, from 1835 until 1882. He wrote a great many part songs, hymns, and anthems. Of these, *Come Ye Thankful People* has retained its currency.

EMMETT, Daniel Decatur, American composer of *Dixie* and other regional songs and ballads. He was born in Mt. Vernon, Ohio, October 29, 1815, and died there, June 28, 1904. He sang and played the banjo in minstrel groups. In 1859 he wrote the words and the music of *Dixie,* which paradoxically became the fighting song of the South during the Civil War even though its composer was a Northerner.

EXNER, Max, American composer. He was born in Shanghai, China, January 13, 1910. Coming to America as a youth, he studied music at Columbia University (M.A., 1946). In 1947 he was appointed extension specialist in music at Iowa State University at Ames. Since 1948 he also has held the position of director of music at United Church of Christ there. He has published a number of choral pieces, among them *Now All the Woods are Waking, I Have a Dream, Where Shall I Find the Christ Child?, Glories of His Hand,* etc.

EZELL, Helen Ingle, American pianist and composer. She was born in Marshall, Oklahoma, May 18, 1903. After graduation from Oklahoma City University, she went to New York where she studied composition with Henry Cowell and Otto Luening at Columbia University. She writes mostly for piano. Her teaching pieces are programmatic: *Barn Dance, Day in Spring, Going Somewhere?, Hop o' My Thumb, Wind through the Trees,* etc.

FALLA, Manuel de, one of the greatest composers of modern Spain. He was born in Cádiz, November 23, 1876, and died in Alta Gracia, in the province of Córdoba, Argentina, November 14, 1946. He was a pupil of Felipe Pedrell in Madrid, and as a youth wrote zarzuelas. In 1907 he went to Paris. Under the influence of the modern French School he adopted the technique of Impressionism without sacrificing the Spanish character of his melodic and rhythmic inspiration. His ballets *El Amor brujo* (1915) and *El Sombrero de tres picos* (1919) became enormously popular. He also made arrangements of Spanish and Catalan folksongs.

FARNABY, Giles, English composer. He was born in Truro, Cornwall, about 1560, and died in London in 1640. His virginal pieces and madrigals, written in a fine contrapuntal manner, enjoyed excellent success.

FAURÉ, Gabriel, great French composer and educator. He was born in Pamiers, Ariège, May 12, 1845, and died in Paris, November 4, 1924. Fauré was a pupil of Saint-Saëns, served as organist in various churches in Paris, and in 1896 was appointed chief organist at the Madeleine. At the same time he joined the staff of the Paris Conservatory and later was its director from 1905 till 1920. In many respects, Fauré anticipated the techniques of Impressionism, particularly in his evocative use of modality and consecutive triadic progressions. His songs are models of modern French vocal art, and his instrumental pieces are distinguished by impeccable precision of polyphonic structure.

FIBICH, Zdenko, Czech composer. He was born in Seborice, December 21, 1850, and died in Prague, October 15, 1900. He studied in Leipzig. His most popular piece is *Poème* for piano, marked by an ingratiating melody set in chromatic harmonies.

FIELD, John, Irish pianist and composer. He was born in Dublin, July 26, 1782, and died in Moscow, January 23, 1837. He studied with Clementi and in 1803 went to Russia as a teacher. He wrote mainly for piano. His historical importance lies in the undeniable influence he exercised on Chopin, Field having been the first to develop the genre of the piano nocturne.

FISCHER, Johann Kaspar Ferdinand, German composer of keyboard music. He was born about 1665 and died in 1746. He was attached to the court of the Margrave of Baden from 1696 to 1716. In 1715 he published a collection of twenty preludes and fugues for organ in twenty different keys, which closely anticipated Bach's *Well-tempered Clavier.* Fischer wrote a great number of keyboard pieces in classical forms, of which *Passacaille en Rondeau* is a typical example.

FOSTER, Stephen C., American composer of popular ballads. He was born in Lawrenceville, Pittsburgh, July 4, 1826, and died in New York, January 13, 1864. He had no professional training in music, but possessed a unique gift for writing ballads imbued with the spirit of the American countryside. Of these the most popular are *Camptown Races, Come Where My Love Lies Dreaming, Jeanie with the Light Brown Hair, My Old Kentucky Home, Oh! Susanna, Old Black Joe,* and *The Old Folks at Home (Swanee River).* Foster's last song, written in 1864, was *Beautiful Dreamer.*

FRACKENPOHL, Arthur, American composer. He was born in Irvington, New Jersey, April 23, 1924. He studied at the Eastman School of Music in Rochester (B.A., 1947; M.A., 1949) and at McGill University in Montreal, Canada (Mus. Doc., 1957). His principal teachers of composition were Bernard Rogers at the Eastman School and Nadia Boulanger in France. He was awarded several prizes and grants. Eventually he became professor at the State University College in Potsdam, New York. He wrote many teaching pieces for piano.

FRANKE, Theodore, 19th-century German composer of light music. He settled in Russia as teacher and composer; his instrumental *Intermezzo Russe* warrants mention.

FRANZ, Robert, German song composer. He was born in Halle, June 28, 1815, and died there, October 24, 1892. He studied in Dessau, but returned to Halle shortly afterwards as an organist at the principal church. Later he taught at Halle University. Like Beethoven and Smetana, Franz was afflicted with deafness. He wrote some 350 songs, among them some of the finest examples of the German Lied.

FRESCOBALDI, Girolamo, great Italian organist and composer. He was born in Ferrara in September 1583, and died in Rome, March 1, 1643. He travelled to the Netherlands and published his early works in Antwerp. In 1608 he was appointed organist of St. Peter's in Rome, holding this post until his death. His keyboard pieces are remarkable for their contrapuntal ingenuity.

FROBERGER, Johann Jakob, famous German organist. He was born in Stuttgart, May 18, 1616, and died in Héricourt, Haute-Saône, France, May 7,1667. In 1637 he went to Rome where he became a student of Frescobaldi. He was probably the first to establish the traditional order of dances in a Classical suite (Allemande, Courante, Sarabande, Gigue).

FULMER, H. J., American lyricist whose real name was Charles E. Pratt. The song *My Bonnie Lies Over the Ocean* was attributed to him in a sheet music edition published in New York in 1882. The first printing of this song appeared in a collection of students' songs, published in Cambridge, Massachusetts, in 1881.

GADE, Niels V., Danish composer, one of the founders

of the National Scandinavian School. He was born in Copenhagen, February 22, 1817, and died there, December 21, 1890. Like many Scandinavian composers of the nineteenth century, he wrote songs to German texts. Later he went to Leipzig where he formed an intimate friendship with Mendelssohn. He undoubtedly experienced a profound influence of German music, but he succeeded in injecting a national flavor into the familiar forms. His piano pieces *Spring Flowers, Aquarelles, Idylls*, and others retain their popularity.

GANNE, Louis, French composer. He was born in Buxières-les-Mines, Allier, April 5, 1862, and died in Paris, July 13, 1923. He studied with Massenet at the Paris Conservatory, and was active as ballet conductor in Paris and Monte Carlo. He also composed a number of symphonic dances of which *La Czarina*, in various arrangements, became popular.

GAUTIER, Leonard, French composer of light instrumental music. His *Le Secret (Intermezzo Pizzicato)* became popular.

GEORGE, Earl, American composer and pianist. He was born in Milwaukee, Wisconsin, May 1, 1924. He studied at the Eastman School of Music in Rochester (B.M., 1946; M.M., 1947; Ph.D., 1948), won numerous awards and grants, and held a Guggenheim Fellowship in 1957. He has written effective teaching pieces for piano, among them *At Bedtime, The Ballerina, Chicken Feed, Copy-Cat, Drifting Clouds, Hopscotch.*

GERMAN, Sir Edward, English composer. He was born in Whitchurch, Shropshire, February 17, 1862, and died in London, November 11, 1936. He studied at the Royal Academy of Music and wrote a symphony at his graduation. Subsequently he devoted himself to the composition of theater music. His most successful work was *Dance Suite* from incidental music to the play *Henry VIII*. His real name was Edward German Jones.

GHIS, Henri, French pianist and composer. He was born in Toulon, May 17, 1839, and died in Paris, April 24, 1908. He studied at the Paris Conservatory. Later he published a number of salon dances. He achieved fame solely on the strength of his piano arrangement of *Amaryllis*, an old French melody, which he published under the title *Air de Louis XIII.*

GIARDINI, Felice de', Italian violinist and composer. He was born in Turin, April 12, 1716, and died in Moscow, June 8, 1796. He studied singing and violin, played in theater orchestras in Italy, then joined the Italian opera in London as conductor. In 1796 he was engaged as violinist and composer by the Russian court of Catherine II, but died shortly upon arrival in Russia.

GILLET, Ernest, French composer. He was born in Paris, September 13, 1856, and died there, May 6, 1940. He studied cello at the Paris Conservatory. He published a number of salon pieces for piano, of which *Loin du Bal* enjoys perennial popularity.

GILLOCK, William L., American pianist and composer. He was born in Lawrence County, Missouri, July 1, 1917. He studied piano at Central Methodist College in Fayette, Missouri. Upon graduation he taught piano privately in New Orleans. In 1967 he moved to Dallas, Texas. Gillock composed about 300 piano pieces, among them *Autumn is Here, Happy Holiday,* and *The Prowling Pussy Cat.* He has also published a manual, *Piano All the Way.*

GILMORE, Patrick S., American bandmaster and composer. He was born in County Galway, Ireland, December 25, 1829, and died in St. Louis, September 24, 1892. After travelling in Canada with an English band, he settled in New England in 1859 and organized Gilmore's Band. He took part in the National Peace Jubilee in 1869 and the World's Peace Jubilee in 1872. He published the famous Civil War song *When Johnny Comes Marching Home* under the pseudonym Louis Lambert in 1863.

GLINKA, Mikhail Ivanovich, great Russian composer, called "Father of Russian Music." He was born in Novosspaskoye, near Smolensk, June 1, 1804, and died in Berlin, February 15, 1857. He was virtually self-taught in composition, but studied singing and violin in St. Petersburg. In 1830 he went to Italy and in 1833 he proceeded to Berlin where he took a course in composition with Dehn. Returning to Russia, he produced the national opera *A Life for the Czar* in St. Petersburg, on December 9, 1836, and the event became a landmark of Russian music. His second opera, *Russlan and Ludmilla,* produced six years later, was a fairy-tale. Glinka also wrote some symphonic music and a number of songs which are distinguished by their unaffected melodic quality.

GLUCK, Christoph Willibald von, great Austrian operatic composer. He was born in Erasbach, in the Upper Palatinate, July 2, 1714, and died in Vienna, November 15, 1787. After receiving elementary instruction, he played violin and sang in church choirs. In 1736 he was chamber musician to Prince Lobkowitz in Vienna, and in 1737 he went to Italy to complete his education with G. B. Sammartini. He produced several Italian operas, and in 1745 he went to London as conductor of Italian opera. Returning to Vienna, he premiered his masterpiece, *Orfeo ed Euridice,* on October 5, 1762. His fame spread, and he was invited to Paris. There he produced *Armide* on September 23, 1777, and *Iphigénie en Tauride* on May 18, 1779. The historic operatic rivalry between Gluck and the Italian composer Nicola Piccinni aroused passions among adherents of the "dramatic opera" promulgated by Gluck and those following the Italian practice of music for theatrical entertainment. Gluck, to whom this polemical strife was repugnant, returned to Vienna.

GODARD, Benjamin, French composer. He was born in Paris, August 18, 1849, and died in Cannes, January 10, 1895. He studied at the Paris Conservatory. His talent expressed itself best in lyric opera. After the production of two early operas with indifferent success, he wrote his masterpiece, *Jocelyn,* after a poem by Lamartine, which was staged in Brussels, February 25, 1888. The *Berceuse* from this opera became a perennial favorite.

GOSSEC, François-Joseph, Belgian composer. He was born in Vergnies, January 17, 1734, and died in Paris, February 16, 1829. He studied organ and violin and was a chorister at the Antwerp Cathedral. In 1751 he settled in Paris where he gained favor with influential members of the royal aristocracy. He occupied a variety of important posts and succeeded in retaining his status after the Revolution. He produced a number of successful operas under the old regime; adopting the dramatic reforms of Lully, he enhanced the dynamic and instrumental resources in his scores. To celebrate the Revolution, he wrote choral works requiring the participation of large masses of singers and instrumentalists. He was also a master of chamber music, and he wrote some engaging dances in the French manner.

GOULD, Morton, American composer and conductor. He was born in Richmond Hill, New York, December 10, 1913. He studied piano with Abby Whiteside and theory with Vincent Jones. Subsequently he attended the Institute of Musical Art and New York University. While still a very young man, he appeared as pianist and composer in radio concerts. Later he was a frequent guest conductor of major American orchestras and made records of his own compositions as well as those of other American composers. His works include four symphonies, *Chorale and Fugue in Jazz* for two pianos and orchestra, concertos for piano, for violin, for orchestra, for four pianos and orchestra, and a unique concerto for tap dancer and orchestra in which the dancing rhythm determines the thematic content. His *Latin American Symphonette* and three *American Symphonettes* achieved considerable popularity.

GOUNOD, Charles, celebrated French opera composer. He was born in Paris, June 17, 1818, and died there, October 18, 1893. He was a student of Halévy at the Paris Conservatory, and in 1839 graduated with the Grand Prix de Rome. Gounod produced three operas which were only moderately well received. Then, on March 19, 1859, came the production at the Théâtre-Lyrique in Paris of his masterpiece, *Faust,* after Goethe's poem. Its success was universal. Gounod's orchestral miniature *Funeral March of a Marionette,* composed in 1873, became famous in motion pictures and television as the musical theme of Alfred Hitchcock's crime mysteries. In 1853 Gounod wrote a violin solo superimposed on the first prelude of Bach's *Well-tempered Clavier,* which was later arranged as a song with the Latin words of the prayer *Ave Maria.*

GRANADOS, Enrique, national Spanish composer. He was born in Lérida, July 27, 1867, and died at sea, March 24, 1916, when the ship S.S. Sussex on which he was a passenger was sunk by a German submarine in the English Channel. He was a student of Felipe Pedrell in Madrid, played piano in restaurants and cabarets, then began composing zarzuelas. His major work is *Goyescas,* inspired by scenes from the paintings of Goya and originally written as a piano suite. He also wrote a great number of separate pieces in the Spanish vein. Later Granados used the material of *Goyescas* for an opera (with the same name), which was first produced at the Metropolitan Opera in New York, January 28, 1916, in the presence of the composer. It was after his return to Europe that he perished.

GRAUN, Karl Heinrich, German opera composer. He was born in Wahrenbrück, near Dresden, May 7, 1704, and died in Berlin, August 8, 1759. He was a singer and an organist. In 1725 he sang in opera at the Brunswick court and then began himself to compose operas to Italian librettos. He also adopted the Italian operatic style of set arias. In addition, he was a prolific composer of instrumental music.

GREGH, Louis, French composer and publisher. He was born in Philippeville, Algeria, March 16, 1843, and died at St. Mesme, Seine-et-Oise, January 21, 1915. He wrote operettas and ballets before turning to music publishing. Several of his light pieces have achieved a certain popularity.

GRIEG, Edvard, celebrated Norwegian composer. He was born in Bergen, June 15, 1843, and died there, September 4, 1907. His family stemmed from Scotland, and his ancestral name was Greig. He studied at the Leipzig Conservatory and became imbued with the essence of German Romanticism. In 1863 he went to Copenhagen where he studied briefly with Niels Gade. Returning to Norway in 1867, he became determined to create a national School of Scandinavian music. His greatest accomplishment was the music he wrote in 1873 for Ibsen's *Peer Gynt,* and from which he extracted two instrumental suites. The combination of Norwegian folkways and German Romanticism in his music resulted in an individual lyric style of superb definition.

GRIFFES, Charles Tomlinson, American pianist and composer, preeminent in the Impressionist style. He was born in Elmira, New York, September 17, 1884, and died in New York, April 8, 1920. He studied piano and organ with local teachers. In 1903 he went to Berlin where he studied composition with Engelbert Humperdinck. In 1907 he returned to the United States to become a teacher at the Hackley School for Boys in Tarrytown, New York. He is best known for his *Roman Sketches* for piano (which include *The White Peacock* and *The Fountains of Acqua Paola*). It is the most enduring work in an authentic Impressionist style by an American composer. He also wrote the symphonic tone poem *The Pleasure Dome of Kubla Khan.* A hitherto unpublished work, *Legend,* appears for the first time in the New Scribner Music Library; it was discovered by Miss Donna K. Anderson and is reproduced here with the permission of the sisters of Charles Griffes.

GRUBER, Edmund, American composer. He was born in Cincinnati in 1879 and died at Fort Leavenworth, Kansas, in 1941. In 1907, in the Philippine Islands, he wrote the words and music of *The Caissons Go Rolling Along* for the 5th Artillery, to celebrate the reunion of two sections of his regiment. It became the official artillery song of the U.S. Army. John Philip Sousa arranged it for military band in 1918.

GRUBER, Franz, Austrian composer and organist who wrote the famous Christmas carol *Stille Nacht, Heilige Nacht.* He was born in Unterweizburg, November 25, 1787, and died in Hallein, near Salzburg, June 7, 1863. He earned his living as an organist and school teacher. He composed his celebrated carol on Christmas Eve, 1818, to the words of the local curate, Joseph Mohr.

HAHN, Reynaldo, Venezuelan-born French composer. He was born in Caracas, August 9, 1875, and died in Paris, January 28, 1947. He was taken to Paris as an infant. There he studied composition with Massenet. Hahn composed mainly vocal music; his light operas have a distinctly Parisian flair. Some of his chansons have become popular in song recitals.

HANBY, Benjamin Russell, American song writer and preacher. He was born in Rushville, Ohio, in 1833 and died in Westerville, Ohio, in 1867. He was a sophomore at Otterbein College, Westerville, Ohio, when he wrote the anti-slavery song *Darling Nelly Gray*, which achieved immense popularity in the abolition movement. It is said that the song is a true story which Hanby heard from a fugitive slave named Joseph Selby.

HANDEL, George Frideric, one of the greatest composers of the Baroque period, second in importance only to J. S. Bach. He was born in Halle, February 23, 1685, and died in London, April 14, 1759. He played the organ as a child. In 1706 he travelled to Italy. Returning to Germany, he became court musician to the Elector of Hannover, who later assumed the throne of England as George I. Handel settled in London and eventually became a British subject. After a failure to gain social and financial support for his operatic enterprise in London, he turned to the composition of oratorios to English texts, a felicitous development climaxed by the production of his immortal *Messiah* in 1742. Handel also wrote numerous instrumental works. All of his compositions are marked by supreme mastery of counterpoint; in fact, the formal perfection of his music set a standard for British composers to emulate.

HANSON, Howard, eminent American composer, conductor, and educator. He was born in Wahoo, Nebraska, October 28, 1896, and received his early musical training from his mother. Later, he studied at Luther Junior College in Wahoo and at the Institute of Musical Art in New York. After graduation from Northwestern University in 1916, he joined the staff of the College of the Pacific. In 1921 he won the Prix de Rome of the American Academy there. In 1924 he was appointed by George Eastman as director of the Eastman School of Music in Rochester, a post he held for forty years, until 1964. Two generations of American composers were his students. He also organized festivals of American music there, at which he conducted a number of orchestral concerts. In 1961 he travelled with the Eastman School Orchestra in seventeen countries, including Russia, under the auspices of the State Department. Hanson is the recipient of many awards, including the Pulitzer Prize. He has been president of the National Association of Schools of Music, the Music Teachers National Association, and the National Music Council. Among his many works are six symphonies, the opera *Merry Mount* commissioned by the Metropolitan Opera Company, choral pieces, and chamber music. He published an innovative manual, *Harmonic Materials of Modern Music* (1960). He is the editor-in-chief of the New Scribner Music Library. (*For additional biographical information see Volume 1.*)

HARRISON, Annie Fortescue, English composer of light music. She was born in 1851 and died in 1944 at the age of ninety-three. In 1877 she married Lord Arthur Hill, the comptroller of Queen Victoria's household. In the same year, at the age of 26, she published her piano piece entitled *In the Gloaming*, which became a perennial favorite on both sides of the Atlantic.

HARTHAN, Hans, German-born pianist and composer. He was born in Bavaria, Feb. 23, 1855, and died in Glendale, California, March 14, 1936. He studied in Munich with Lachner and Reinberger, then became orchestra and chorus conductor in Magdeburg. In 1883 he went to Russia and was professor of music in Odessa and in Dorpat. From 1896 to 1901 he was director of the National Conservatory of Music in Santiago, Chile. In 1903 he came to the United States at the invitation of the Philadelphia Singing Society. Later he settled in California. He wrote orchestral, vocal, and instrumental music of various descriptions, as well as numerous piano works—all of them marked by excellent craftsmanship.

HASSLER, Hans Leo, German composer, one of the founders of the National Music School of Germany. He was born in Nuremberg, October 25, 1564, and died in Frankfurt, June 8, 1612. After receiving rudimentary training with his father, he went to Venice where he became a student of Andrea Gabrieli. Returning to Germany, he served as organist to the Elector of Saxony in Dresden, and later followed him to Frankfurt. In his compositions, Hassler cultivated the formative elements of German folksongs and dances, but arranged them according to traditional Italian counterpoint. His sacred works and madrigals are significant landmarks in the historic evolution of German music.

HASTINGS, Thomas, American hymn composer. He was born in Litchfield, Connecticut, October 15, 1784, and died in New York, May 15, 1872. He wrote more than one thousand hymn tunes, but his fame rests on the perennial favorite, *Rock of Ages*, to the text by Augustus Toplady, which was published in 1831.

HATTON, John, English hymn composer. Biographical information on him is lacking, except for the year of his death, 1793. He wrote *Jesus Shall Reign Where'er the Sun*.

HAUSER, Miska, Hungarian violinist. He was born in Pressburg in 1822 and died in Vienna, December 8, 1887. He became a virtuoso performer and toured Europe, the United States, South America, and Australia. His violin pieces enjoyed considerable success.

HAYDN, Joseph, great Austrian composer, founder of the Classical School of composition. He was born in Rohrau-on-the-Leitha, in Lower Austria, March 31, 1732, and died in Vienna, May 31, 1809. At the age of eight he was taken to Vienna where he became chorister at St. Stephen's Cathedral. He acquired the knowledge of composition from perusing *Gradus ad Parnassum* by Fux and received further musical instruction from Porpora. A decisive event in Haydn's life was his engagement by the Prince Esterházy as music director at the latter's estate in Eisenstadt. After the death of the prince, Haydn remained in the service of his brother. Free from pecuniary preoccupations, Haydn devoted his energies to composition and performance. In 1791 he travelled to England, and in 1794 he made a second trip there. Upon his return to Austria, he remained in Vienna. Haydn's social status was greatly enhanced in 1797, when he wrote the national Austrian anthem, *Gott erhalte Franz den Kaiser*. The same tune was used in 1841 for the German patriotic song *Deutschland über Alles*. Haydn is popularly known as "the father of the symphony," and indeed, he brought the Classical symphonic form to the heights of perfection. He can be described with equal justice as the father of the string quartet. The number of symphonies ascribed to Haydn is at least one hundred and four; the number of his string quartets is in the vicinity of eighty. Haydn also composed many concertos and pieces of chamber music of various descriptions, as well as oratorios and other vocal works. His numerous keyboard compositions include over fifty sonatas.

HELLER, Stephen, famous Hungarian pianist and composer. He was born in Budapest, May 15, 1813, and died in Paris, January 14, 1888. He studied in Vienna and began touring Europe as a pianist at the age of fifteen. In 1838 he went to Paris where he entered the circle of celebrated contemporaries, among them Chopin and Liszt. He composed salon pieces for piano; the best of them approached a very high degree of musical excellence. His *Tarantella* and some of his piano etudes still retain their merited place in the piano repertory.

HELMORE, Thomas, English hymn composer. He was born in 1811 and died in 1890. His hymn tune *O Come, O Come, Emmanuel* is included in many services.

HEMY, Henri Frederick, English organist and hymn writer. He was born, of German parents, in Newcastle-on-Tyne, November 12, 1818, and died in Hartlepool in 1888. He served as a church organist in England. In 1864 he compiled an anthology, *Crown of Jesus Music*. Among his hymn tunes, *Faith of Our Fathers* is a standard in congregational usage.

HENRY VIII, the renowned English King and beheader of two queens was born in Greenwich, June 28, 1491, and died in Windsor, January 28, 1547. He was educated musically and wrote sacred and secular music. His *Kynge's Maske* is notable.

HERBERT, Victor, one of the greatest composers of light operas. He was born in Dublin, Ireland, February 1, 1859, and died in New York, May 26, 1924. He studied cello in Germany and played in various European bands. In 1886 he joined the orchestra of the Metropolitan Opera in New York as a cellist. At that same time he began to compose. He also conducted army bands. He was the regular conductor of the Pittsburgh Symphony Orchestra from 1898 to 1904. His attempts at grand opera were unsuccessful, but his operettas, which he began to put out in 1894, were increasingly popular. Among separate numbers, *Kiss Me Again* became a perennial favorite.

HILTON, John (the Younger), English madrigal composer. He was born in Oxford in 1599 and died in London, March 21, 1657. He served as organist at St. Margaret's, Westminster, beginning in 1628. He published a collection of airs, catches, rounds, and canons.

HOLDEN, Oliver, American hymn writer. He was born in Shirley, Massachusetts, September 18, 1765, and died in Charlestown, Massachusetts, September 4, 1844. He was variously employed as a justice of the peace, carpenter, preacher, and was a member of the State House of Representatives. He also sold music and gave singing lessons. His best hymn tune, *Coronation*, to the words *All Hail the Power of Jesus' Name*, was published in his *Union Harmony* in 1793.

HOLLAENDER, Viktor, German composer. He was born in Leobschütz, April 20, 1866, and died in Hollywood, October 24, 1940. He was active as a theater conductor in Berlin until 1933, when he emigrated to America and settled in Los Angeles. He wrote several light operas, songs, and piano pieces.

HOPKINS, John Henry, American churchman and hymnologist. He was born in Pittsburgh, October 28, 1820, and died near Hudson, New York, August 13, 1891. He was trained for the ministry, served as deacon and rector in several churches, and published several anthologies of carols and hymns. His song *We Three Kings of Orient Are* has become a popular Christmas carol.

HOPKINSON, Francis, American statesman, signer of the Declaration of Independence. He was born in Philadelphia, September 21, 1737, and died there, May 9, 1791. He was an amateur musician and is generally regarded as the composer of the first original American song, *My Days Have Been so Wondrous Free*, which was written in 1759. In the foreword to his collection of tunes for a keyboard instrument, dedicated to George Washington and published in 1788, he states explicitly: "I cannot, I believe, be refused the credit of being the first native of the United States who has produced a musical composition."

HOWARD, John Tasker, American composer and writer on music. He was born in Brooklyn, November 30, 1890, and died in West Orange, New Jersey, November 20, 1964. He attended Williams College and upon graduation engaged in musical journalism. He was curator of the Americana Music Collection at the New York Public Library (1940–56). His book *Our American Music*, first published in 1929, was a pioneering work in the field and has been reprinted numerous times. He also published an important monograph on Stephen Foster. Howard composed music in a romantic manner and also made effective piano arrangements of American songs and dance tunes.

HOWE, Mary, American pianist and composer. She was born in Richmond, Virginia, April 4, 1882, and died in Washington, D.C., September 14, 1964. She studied at the Peabody Conservatory in Baltimore with Ernest Hutcheson (piano) and Gustav Strube (composition). In 1915 she moved to Washington where she became active in cultural and educational fields. She wrote many choral works and several orchestral pieces, as well as chamber music.

HULL, Anne, American pianist. She was born in Brookland, Pennsylvania, January 25, 1888. She studied music at the Peabody Conservatory in Baltimore; her teachers were Ernest Hutcheson in piano and Otis B. Boise in theory. Upon graduation she devoted herself to piano pedagogy. She was on the faculty in the preparatory department of the Peabody Conservatory from 1910 to 1923; on the faculty of Greenwich House Music School in New York from 1923 to 1938; and at the Juilliard School of Music in New York from 1940 to 1967. In 1965 she received a citation for distinguished service to music from the Peabody Alumni Association. For many years she appeared as a duo pianist with Mary Howe and wrote special works for her concerts. Of these, *Ancient Ballad* enjoyed a special popularity. She also published a number of teaching pieces for piano.

ILYINSKY, Alexander, Russian composer. He was born in Tsarskoye Selo, January 24, 1859, and died in Moscow, February 23, 1920. He studied in Berlin. Returning to Russia, he was active mainly as a teacher. He published some character pieces for piano and other instruments, as well as songs.

IVANOVICI, Ion, Rumanian composer of popular music. He was born in Bucharest, in 1845, and died there, September 29, 1902. He was a band leader and published 150 numbers for band. Of these, *The Waves of the Danube*, which he wrote in 1880, became universally popular.

IVES, Charles E., the most original American composer of the twentieth century, whose works combine a profoundly expressed spirit of the nation with astoundingly prophetic insights into modern techniques. He was born in Danbury, Connecticut, October 20, 1874, and died in New York, May 19, 1954. His father was a bandleader of the First Connecticut Heavy Artillery during the Civil War, and Charles Ives played drums in his father's band. Soon he began to compose band tunes himself. He then entered Yale University where he studied composition with Horatio Parker and organ with Dudley Buck. Upon graduation, he was employed as a clerk in an insurance company, and in 1907 he formed a partnership with Julian Myrick. Ives showed remarkable ability to conduct business, and the Ives & Myrick insurance company prospered. In 1908 he married Harmony Twichell. Ives continued to compose symphonic, vocal, and instrumental music of unique originality and ingenuity. In 1919 he published, at his own expense, his *Concord Sonata* for piano, a work of truly epoch-making significance, and in 1921 he brought out a volume of 114 songs; he distributed these publications free of charge to anyone desiring to own copies. Of his orchestral works, the grandiose *Fourth Symphony* was not performed in its entirety until several years after his death. In 1947 he received the Pulitzer Prize for his *Third Symphony* written in 1911. While only a handful of performers and commentators evinced any serious interest in his works during his lifetime, an extraordinary revival of his music took place not only in America but also in Europe as the realization of his importance dawned upon the music world. Although his works pose tremendous technical difficulties for performance, their popularity in concerts and in recordings continues to grow. The most ingratiating musical trait of Ives is perhaps his ability to weave into the complex fabric of his music fragments of old American hymn tunes, dances, and once-popular ballads, and his intuitive ability to invent melodies that possess an authentic folklike flavor.

JENSEN, Adolf, German composer of songs. He was born in Königsberg, January 12, 1837, and died in Baden-Baden, January 23, 1879. He was variously active as a theater conductor and a teacher in Germany. For a while, he studied with Niels Gade in Copenhagen. Jensen wrote a great many songs closely emulating the Romantic Lieder type, and also some piano pieces in Schumann's manner.

JUON, Paul, Russian composer. He was born in Moscow, March 6, 1872, and died in Vevey, Switzerland, August 21, 1940. He studied composition in Moscow with Taneyev and Arensky. In 1906 he settled in Berlin as teacher and composer. He cultivated a Romantic type of composition and wrote a great deal of chamber music and stylized dances for various instruments.

KILPATRICK, Jack Frederick, American composer of partly Cherokee Indian extraction. He was born in Stillwater, Oklahoma, September 23, 1915, and died in Dallas, Texas, in 1967. He attended the University of Redlands, California, and later, Catholic University in Washington, D.C. From 1946 until his death he was composer in residence at Southern Methodist University in Dallas, Texas. He wrote effective piano pieces with story-telling titles (*The Ant-Soldiers, The Fifer of Bunker Hill, The Lazy Boat, The Singing Top,* etc.).

KJERULF, Halfdan, Norwegian composer. He was born in Oslo, September 15, 1815, and died in its vicinity,

August 11, 1868. He went to Leipzig for his musical education, returning to Norway in 1851. He wrote more than one hundred songs and several collections of piano pieces, all imbued with the Romantic spirit and closely following the traditional forms. Like Grieg after him, Kjerulf injected an element of Scandinavian dance rhythms and melodic inflections into his compositions, which made them distinct from their German models.

KLEINMICHEL, Richard, German pianist and composer. He was born in Posen, December 31, 1846, and died in Charlottenburg, August 18, 1901. He studied with his father, a bandmaster, and later took courses at the Leipzig Conservatory. He eventually became active as theater conductor. Kleinmichel wrote mostly in small forms and published a number of characteristic pieces for piano. His signal accomplishment was to arrange the entire *Ring des Nibelungen* for piano.

KNIGHT, Joseph Philip, English cleric and song composer. He was born in Bradford-on-Avon, July 26, 1812, and died at Great Yarmouth, June 2, 1887. He studied organ and began to compose hymns as a youth. While on a mission in the U.S. in 1839, he wrote his celebrated tune *Rocked in the Cradle of the Deep.*

KODÁLY, Zoltán, famous Hungarian composer, founder, in close association with Béla Bartók, of the modern Hungarian School of Composition. He was born in Kecskemet, December 16, 1882, and died in Budapest, March 6, 1967. He studied with Hans Koessler at the Budapest Academy of Music and later took lessons with Widor in Paris. Returning to Hungary, he embarked with Bartók on a systematic codification of Hungarian folksongs and travelled through the countryside in search of authentic material. He also became active in the educational field and devised a method of solfeggio that has become universally established as the Kodály Method. Virtually all of his works are permeated with Hungarian song inflections. In 1923 he wrote a *Psalmus Hungaricus* to commemorate the half century of the union of Buda and Pest. His orchestral arrangements of Hungarian folk dances are distinguished by both authenticity and modernity. His comic opera *Háry János* enjoys great popularity.

KÖHLER, Louis, German piano pedagogue and composer. He was born in Brunswick, September 5, 1820, and died in Königsberg, February 16, 1886. He studied piano and composition in Vienna. In 1847 he settled in Königsberg where he established a music school. He wrote a number of characteristic piano pieces in a Romantic manner, but his main claim to fame is his systematic method of piano study.

KRAMER, A. Walter, American music editor and composer. He was born in New York, September 23, 1890, and died there, April 8, 1969. He studied at the College of the City of New York. Upon graduation, he devoted himself to musical journalism. He was editor in chief of *Musical America* from 1929 to 1936; he also held posts with publishing houses. Kramer was a prolific composer; his published works number about three hundred. His songs and piano pieces are written in an effective style, suitable for teaching or concert performance.

KÜCKEN, Friedrich, German composer and conductor. He was born in Bleckede, November 16, 1810, and died in Schwerin, April 3, 1882. He studied in Berlin and Vienna, and was a theater conductor in Stuttgart from 1851 until 1861. He wrote two operas and some chamber music, but he is principally renowned for his romantic Lieder.

KUHLAU, Friedrich, German composer. He was born in Ülzen, September 11, 1786, and died in Copenhagen, March 12, 1832. He settled in Copenhagen as a youth in order to evade conscription into Napoleon's army. In 1813 he was appointed music director at the Danish court. He produced several operas in Copenhagen and much chamber music, but his name is chiefly known because of his piano sonatinas which are melodically and harmonically ingratiating and not difficult to play.

KUHNAU, Johann, German composer, Bach's predecessor at the Thomaskirche in Leipzig. He was born in Geising, April 6, 1660, and died in Leipzig, June 5, 1722. He studied in Dresden and Leipzig and became musical director of the University of Leipzig in 1700 and cantor at the Thomaskirche in 1701. He was succeeded in that post by Bach. Kuhnau's historical importance rests on his attempt to write programmatic music for instruments. His *Bible Stories in Six Sonatas* for keyboard are unique.

KULLAK, Theodor, famous German pianist and teacher. He was born in Krotoschin, September 12, 1818, and died in Berlin, March 1, 1882. He studied music theory with Dehn in Berlin and piano with Czerny in Vienna. In 1850 he established a music school in Berlin, with Julius Stern and Bernhard Marx as codirectors. He dissolved the partnership in 1855 and organized Kullak's Academy. He published a number of characteristic pieces for piano and manuals of piano technique.

LACK, Théodore, French pianist and composer. He was born in Quimper, Finistère, September 3, 1846, and died in Paris, November 25, 1921. He studied piano with Marmontel at the Paris Conservatory. Upon graduation, he was appointed a piano instructor there and held this post for fifty-seven years until his death. His piano pieces, written in a facile salon style, have become popular.

LA MONTAINE, John, American composer and pianist. He was born in Oak Park, Illinois, March 17, 1920. He studied piano with Rudolf Ganz in Chicago and composition with Howard Hanson and Bernard Rogers at the Eastman School of Music in Rochester. He also took courses with Nadia Boulanger. He received two Guggenheim Fellowships in composition (1959 and 1960) and the Pulitzer Prize for his *Piano Concerto* in 1959. He is a recipient of numerous commissions from the Ford Foundation and the Koussevitzky Foundation. His Christmas pageant opera *Novellis, Novellis* was produced at the

Washington, D.C. Cathedral on December 24, 1961, as the first part of a trilogy. The second and third sections, *The Shepherds Playe* and *Erode the Great*, were premiered in the Cathedral in 1967 and 1969, respectively.

LAVALLÉE, Calixa, Canadian pianist, author of the French-Canadian anthem. He was born in Verchères, Quebec, December 28, 1842, and died in Boston, January 21, 1891. He studied piano at the Paris Conservatory. Returning to America, he toured as concert pianist. In 1880 he wrote the music of the Canadian national song *O Canada.* He eventually settled in Boston as teacher.

LAVRY, Marc, Israeli composer. He was born in Riga, December 22, 1903, and died in Haifa, March 20, 1967. He studied with Teichmüller at the Leipzig Conservatory and was active as an orchestra conductor in Germany and Sweden. In 1935 he went to Palestine. He was the first to write an opera on a modern Hebrew theme to a libretto in the Hebrew language, *Dan the Guard,* and conducted its first performance in Tel Aviv on February 17, 1945. He wrote two piano concertos and many Hebrew dances for piano on Palestinian themes, some of which are popular.

LEHÁR, Franz, famous Austro-Hungarian composer of light opera. He was born in Komorn, April 30, 1870, and died in Bad Ischl, October 24, 1948. He studied at the Prague Conservatory, played the violin in theater orchestras in Germany and later in Vienna, then conducted military bands. He found his true vocation in the field of light opera. His operetta *Die lustige Witwe* (*The Merry Widow*), produced in Vienna on December 28, 1905, became a sensational success all over the world, and its waltzes are perennial favorites.

LIADOV, Anatol, Russian composer. He was born in St. Petersburg, May 10, 1855, and died on his estate of Polynovka, in the district of Novgorod, August 28, 1914. He was a pupil of Rimsky-Korsakov. In 1878 he was engaged as instructor in theory and harmony at the St. Petersburg Conservatory, and kept this post until his death. Among his students were Prokofiev and Miaskovsky. His source of inspiration was Russian folklore; his symphonic tableaux, *Baba Yaga, Enchanted Lake,* and *Kikimora* are suffused with Russian melodic and rhythmic elements. He also wrote some charming miniatures for piano, among which *Music Box* is a perennial favorite.

LINCOLN, Robert Dix, American pianist and composer. He was born in Woodstock, Ohio, December 3, 1924. After attending the Cincinnati Conservatory of Music (B.M., 1949; M.M., 1950), he went to Paris on a French Government Fellowship and studied with Nadia Boulanger at the Écoles d'Art Américaines (1952) and at the Paris Conservatory (1954–55). Upon his return to the United States, he served on the faculty of East Tennessee State University (1950–57), and in 1957 he was appointed Professor of Music at Douglass College, Rutgers University, New Brunswick, New Jersey. He published some

effective teaching pieces for piano, with descriptive titles (*Bouncing Clowns, Lions and Tigers, The Marching Musicians,* etc.).

LISLE, Rouget de, composer of the *Marseillaise.* He was born in Lons-le-Saulnier, May 10, 1760, and died at Choisy-le-Roy, June 27, 1836. He wrote the famous national hymn in 1792, in Strasbourg, as a patriotic ballad under the title *Chant de guerre pour l'armée du Rhin.* Soldiers marching from Marseilles toward Paris took it up, and this action explains the title. A debate still continues as to whether Rouget de Lisle actually composed the music, but it appears certain that he was the author of the inflammatory words that played such a great role in inspiring the French Revolution.

LISZT, Franz, one of the greatest musicians of the nineteenth century, was superbly endowed as a pianist and composer. He was born in Raiding, Hungary, October 22, 1811, and died in Bayreuth, July 31, 1886. He studied piano with Czerny and composition with Salieri in Vienna. As a child he was introduced to Beethoven. After travelling in Germany, Liszt settled in Paris where he joined the artistic and intellectual élite and formed a close friendship with Chopin. In 1839 he undertook a concert tour through Europe, arousing admiration wherever he went. With Wagner (who later married Liszt's daughter Cosima) he launched an esthetic movement that became known as *Zukunftsmusik* (the music of the future) in which literary, dramatic, and musical elements were to be united in one artistic whole. In accordance with these ideas, Liszt sought musical inspiration in literature and art; such works as *Les Préludes* and the *Faust Symphony* are typical of this preoccupation. His *Hungarian Rhapsodies* for piano are tributes to his ethnic heritage. He advanced the piano technique to the ultimate frontiers of nineteenth-century virtuosity. His power of characterization, both lyric and fantastic, finds its expression in his brilliant piano works *Mephisto Waltz* and *Liebestraum* which are among the best examples of musical Romanticism.

LOEILLET, Jean-Baptiste, member of a Belgian family of musicians. He was born in Ghent, November 18, 1680, and died in London, July 19, 1730. He went to London in 1705 and became a successful music teacher there. He wrote a number of instrumental dances for flute, harpsichord, and other instruments in a traditional Baroque style.

LOEWE, Carl, notable German composer of Lieder. He was born in Löbejün, near Halle, November 30, 1796, and died in Kiel, April 20, 1869. He was a student of theology before dedicating himself to composition. Following the Romantic trend of the times, he wrote German Lieder and ballads; the finest of them are comparable in dramatic power and lyric expression to those of Schubert and Schumann.

LULLY, Jean-Baptiste, famous Florentine composer who made his career in France. He was born in Florence,

November 28, 1632, and died in Paris, March 22, 1687. He was taken to France as a boy, entering the service of Louis XIV. He studied organ and composition in Paris; also organized a band called "les petits violons." In 1662 he was appointed maître de musique at the court of Louis XIV. In his works, he abandoned the Italian method of vocal composition and became an adherent of the more dramatic genre of theater music. He enriched the role of instrumental parts in opera and perfected the definitive form of the French Overture. He elevated the ballet to a new excellence by emphasizing the purely musical elements of the dance tunes. The form of the classical suite owes Lully a historical debt in that he established a symphonically contrasted order of movements.

LUTHER, Martin, the founder of the Protestant movement. He was born in Eisleben, November 10, 1483, and died there, February 18, 1546. He was profoundly versed in music, played the flute, and acquired sufficient theoretical knowledge to compose hymn tunes. It is generally accepted that the great Lutheran hymn *Ein' feste Burg ist unser Gott* (*A Mighty Fortress is Our God*) was indeed composed by Luther.

MACBETH, Allan, Scottish organist and composer. He was born in Greenock, March 13, 1856, and died in Glasgow, August 25, 1910. He studied at the Leipzig Conservatory. Returning to Scotland, he was active as church organist and choral conductor. He wrote several operettas, chamber music, and songs. His *Intermezzo* for strings became popular in programs of light music.

MacDOWELL, Edward, great American composer whose Romantically colored works establish him as the true founder of the American School of composition. He was born in New York, December 18, 1861, and died there, January 23, 1908. He studied piano with Teresa Carreño in New York, Antoine-François Marmontel in Paris, Louis Ehlert in Wiesbaden, and Karl Heymann in Frankfurt. He studied composition with Augustin Savard at the Paris Conservatory and Joachim Raff in Frankfurt. MacDowell stayed in Germany from 1881 until 1888. In 1884 he made a brief trip to America, where he married his former pupil Marian Nevins. From 1888 to 1890 he lived in Boston and played the solo part of his *Piano Concerto* in A Minor with the Boston Symphony Orchestra. His recognition in Europe sufficiently impressed the trustees of Columbia University to appoint him to the first Chair of Music there in 1896. However, difficulties developed in his academic career and he resigned from Columbia University amid controversy. Soon he suffered a mental collapse and spent his last years of life in a pathetic condition. After his death, his widow deeded their summer home in Peterborough, New Hampshire, to the MacDowell Memorial Association, and it became a summer retreat where composers, writers, and other creative artists can live and work. MacDowell wrote mostly instrumental music, excelling in piano works. He composed two piano concertos, four piano sonatas, and a series of ingratiating American suites, *Woodland Sketches, Fireside Tales,* and *New England Idyls.*

MacKOWN, Marjorie, English pianist. She was born in London, April 8, 1896, studied at the London Academy of Music, and eventually settled in the United States. She gave concerts with her husband, Allison MacKown, a cellist. From 1921 to 1957 she taught piano at the Eastman School of Music in Rochester and subsequently joined the staff of the Chatham Laboratory School of Music in Pittsburgh, Pennsylvania.

MADRIGUERA, Enrique, Catalan-American composer. He was born in Barcelona, February 17, 1904. After violin study in Europe he settled in the United States where he organized a Latin American orchestral group. His rhumba *Adiós* achieved great popularity.

MAHLER, Gustav, great Austrian composer and conductor. He was born in Kalischt, Bohemia, July 7, 1860, and died in Vienna, May 18, 1911. He studied piano and composition at the Vienna Conservatory and also took courses in philosophy at the University of Vienna. At the age of twenty he received his first appointment as an opera conductor. After serving for two years as assistant to Arthur Nikisch in Leipzig, he was engaged as music director of the Royal Opera in Budapest where he conducted from 1888 to 1891. He then went to Hamburg as conductor of the City Opera there, remaining at the post until 1897. Finally he received the invitation to be music director at the Vienna Court Opera, one of the most prestigious positions in the theatrical world at the time. During his tenure of ten years (1897–1907) he elevated the standard of performance to new heights, both technically and artistically. He was relentless in achieving his aims, and his reputation both as a disciplinarian and superb interpreter grew. In 1908 he became the principal conductor of the Metropolitan Opera in New York, and in 1909 he was engaged as music director of the New York Philharmonic, attaining in his interpretations an unprecedented excellence. But he ran into the unexpected opposition of an imperious board of women trustees of the orchestra. His health suffered because of physical and mental pressures; he returned to Vienna in the spring of 1911 and died of complications of pneumonia at the age of fifty. His widow, Alma Mahler, openly accused the business management of the New York Philharmonic of precipitating Mahler's death. The greatness of Mahler's symphonies was not recognized during his lifetime. Indeed, they were criticized as diffuse and lacking in dignity; the frequent intercalation of waltz rhythms and folklike tunes and the insertion of solo songs in some movements shocked the traditionalists. The decisive reaffirmation of Mahler's significance as a great composer of the modern era came after his death.

MAKER, Frederick, American hymn writer. He was born in 1844 and died in 1927. Among his hymns, *Dear Lord and Father of Mankind* retains its popularity.

MARIE, Gabriel, French composer of light music. He was born in Paris, January 8, 1852, and died, while traveling in Spain, in Puigcerda, Catalonia, August 29, 1928. He studied at the Paris Conservatory and occupied various posts as a choral conductor. He composed a number

[66]

of semi-Classical melodies and dances of which *La Cinquantaine* became popular.

MARPURG, Friedrich Wilhelm, German composer and writer on music. He was born in Seehausen, Brandenburg, November 21, 1718, and died in Berlin, May 22, 1795. He was a follower of Rameau in theoretical writings and published a number of treatises on the history and theory of music. He also wrote chamber music. Following the example of Rameau and Couperin, he often gave descriptive titles to his keyboard compositions, such as *La Voltigeuse.*

MARSH, Simeon B., American hymn writer. He was born in 1798 and died in 1875. He wrote the tune *Martyn* which was later set to the words *Jesus, Lover of My Soul.*

MASON, Lowell, American organist, composer, and educator. He was born in Medfield, Massachusetts, January 8, 1792, and died in Orange, New Jersey, August 11, 1872. Like most musicians of the early years of the United States, he combined business occupations with music pedagogy and organ playing at churches. He published a number of anthologies of sacred music and wrote hymn tunes of which *Nearer My God to Thee,* composed in 1859, became extremely popular. Mason's son William and grandson Daniel Gregory Mason were also musicians of eminence.

MASSENET, Jules, famous French opera composer. He was born in Montaud, near St.-Etienne, Loire, May 12, 1842, and died in Paris, August 13, 1912. He entered the Paris Conservatory at the age of nine, studied piano and harmony, and received the Grand Prix de Rome in 1863. He was appointed professor of composition at the Paris Conservatory in 1878 and kept his post there until his death. Under the influence of his teacher Ambroise Thomas, he began writing operas. After a few indifferent successes, he produced his early masterpiece *Manon,* which was staged in Paris in 1884. There followed a series of further successes, among them *Werther* (1892), *Thaïs* (1894), and *Don Quichotte* (1910). He also wrote a number of oratorios, several orchestral suites, a great many songs, and piano pieces. Among his popular instrumental pieces is the lyric *Élégie.* It was first published for piano in 1856, and in an arrangement for cello and piano in 1873. In 1875 it was issued as a song to words by Louis Gallet. The *Élégie* epitomizes Massenet's lyric and evocative style of composition, simple in formal structure and ingratiating in melodic and rhythmic content.

McKAY, George Frederick, American composer. He was born in Harrington, Washington, June 11, 1899, and died in Stateline, Nevada, October 4, 1970. He studied at the Eastman School of Music in Rochester with the visiting professors Sinding and Palmgren. After graduation, he went to Seattle and joined the faculty of the University of Washington. A prolific composer, he wrote symphonic and chamber music. His short teaching pieces for piano are couched in an unaffected romantic vein; among the best known are *From the North Woods, Morning Hymn, Spaced Silence, Spiritual,* and *Circling.*

McKINNEY, Mathilde, American pianist. She was born in South Bend, Indiana, January 31, 1904. She attended Oberlin Conservatory and later took piano lessons with Josef and Rosina Lhévinne at the Juilliard School of Music in New York. Her teachers in composition were Marion Bauer and Roy Harris. She subsequently occupied various teaching positions and was on the faculty of Westminster State College in Princeton from 1960 to 1970. She wrote chamber music and a number of piano pieces, among them *Rain Drops, Sad Waltz,* and *Swing Slowly.*

MEDTNER, Nicolai, Russian composer. He was born, of German parents, in Moscow, January 5, 1880, and died in London, November 13, 1951. He studied at the Moscow Conservatory with Safonov (piano) and Taneyev (composition), graduated in 1900, and went on a European tour as pianist. After the Revolution, he left Russia and ultimately settled in London. He appeared as pianist in programs of his own works in the United States in 1924–25 and in 1929–30. Medtner was a Romanticist in his esthetic convictions, derived mainly from Schumann and Liszt. He composed mostly for piano and for voice. He introduced a novel type of instrumental narrative in his series of *Fairy Tales* for piano, written in a free rhapsodic manner, but unified by thematic content.

MEEUWISSE, Willy, Dutch pianist and composer. He was born in Arnhem, December 18, 1914, and died in Amsterdam, August 6, 1952. He studied composition with Sem Dresden in Amsterdam, had a successful career as a concert pianist, and composed a number of works, most of them inspired by the Dutch folkways. His *Suite of Old Dutch Dances* for piano, composed in 1936, is popular.

MENDELSSOHN, Felix, great German composer. He was born in Hamburg, February 3, 1809, and died in Leipzig, November 4, 1847. A scion of a cultural Jewish family, he was brought up in an intellectual atmosphere and displayed versatile talents as a pianist, composer, and scholar at a very early age. He also had a fine talent for painting. His most important teacher was Zelter, from whom he acquired a thorough discipline of instrumental and vocal writing. Mendelssohn embarked on a concert career as a pianist through Europe, and in 1829 he made his first trip to England where he was received with great enthusiasm by royalty, aristocracy, and music lovers at large. He was also active as a symphonic and choral conductor. In 1843 he organized the Leipzig Conservatory and conducted the Gewandhaus concerts in Leipzig. His death at the early age of thirty-eight was greatly lamented all over the world. Mendelssohn was a Romanticist par excellence; his symphonies, his oratorios, his piano concertos, and above all his *Songs Without Words* for piano, express as closely as music can, human moods, impressions of a landscape, or the consciousness of a national essence. His technical expertise approached perfection. While music historians do not regard Mendelssohn as equal to Schumann and Chopin in genius and originality, his music maintains its appeal. *The Wedding March* from Mendelssohn's score to Shakespeare's play *A Midsummer Night's Dream,* composed in 1842, became a nuptial classic.

MILÁN, Luis, Spanish composer. He was born in 1500 and died about 1561. In 1536 he published a manual for learning the six-string guitar, which includes many original villancicos, romanzas, sonetos, etc.

MILLS, Kerry (Frederick Allen), American composer and music publisher. He was born in Philadelphia, February 1, 1869, and died in Hawthorn, California, December 5, 1948. He studied violin, then went to New York in 1896 and engaged in music publishing. He composed a number of songs of which one, *At a Georgia Camp Meeting*, published by his firm in 1897, became popular.

MOLLOY, James Lyman, Irish composer. He was born in King's County, Ireland, August 19, 1837, and died in Henley-on-Thames, England, February 4, 1909. He wrote operettas and numerous separate songs. *Kerry Dance*, usually attributed to Molloy, seems to be, in part at least, taken from an old song, *The Cuckoo*, published in London about 1790. However, his authorship of *Love's Old Sweet Song* is undisputed. It was published in 1884 and achieved immediate popularity.

MOMPOU, Federico, Spanish composer. He was born in Barcelona, April 16, 1893. He studied piano and composition at the Paris Conservatory, lived in Barcelona between 1914 and 1921, in Paris from 1921 until 1941, and then went back to Spain. His piano pieces and songs are fine examples of Spanish modern music.

MONTEVERDI, Claudio, great Italian composer of madrigals and operas. He was born in Cremona, May 15, 1567, and died in Venice, November 29, 1643. He learned music as a choirboy at the Cathedral of Cremona, then worked in the service of the Duke of Mantua. He published a number of collections of madrigals before undertaking the composition of his first operatic work, *Arianna* (1608). In 1613 he became maestro di cappella at San Marco in Venice. There he brought out his dramatic scene *Il Combattimento di Tancredi e Clorinda* (1624). His last opera, *L'Incoronazione di Poppea* (1642), is remarkable for its theatrical effectiveness.

MONTROSE, Percy. Montrose is credited with the composition of *Oh My Darling, Clementine*, which was published in Boston in 1884. However, the words were copyrighted by Oliver Ditson of Boston as early as 1863. Later the title was reduced to *Clementine* and published in 1885 in New York. Nothing is known about the composer, who may have been either American or English.

MOORE, Douglas, eminent American composer and educator. He was born in Cutchogue, New York, August 10, 1893, and died in Greenport, Long Island, New York, July 25, 1969. He studied at Yale University with Horatio Parker and David Stanley Smith (B.M., 1917). Later he went to Paris where he studied organ playing with Charles Tournemire and composition with Vincent d'Indy and Nadia Boulanger. In 1925 he received the Pulitzer Travelling Scholarship in music and spent another year in Europe. In 1926 he became associate professor of music at Columbia University, and in 1940 he succeeded Daniel Gregory Mason as chairman of the Music Department, which post he held until 1962. Moore wrote many orchestral and chamber works, but his most durable composition proved to be the opera on a historic American theme, *The Ballad of Baby Doe*, first produced in 1956. He received the Pulitzer Prize for his opera *Giants in the Earth*. His other operas are *The Devil and Daniel Webster, Wings of a Dove,* and *Carrie Nation*. He also composed teaching pieces for piano.

MORLEY, Thomas, English composer and organist. He was born in 1557 and died in London (?) in 1602. He served as organist at St. Paul's Cathedral in London, published both sacred and popular music, and was the author of the first English music manual, *A Plaine and Easie Introduction to Practicall Musicke* (1597). His songs to English texts retain their historical importance.

MOSZKOWSKI, Moritz, famous German pianist and composer. He was born in Breslau, August 23, 1854, and died in Paris, March 4, 1925. He studied at the Dresden Conservatory and later in Berlin. In 1897 he settled in Paris. His *Serenade* for piano, composed in 1877, and his *Spanish Dances*, also for piano, are standard repertory pieces.

MOZART, Wolfgang Amadeus, great Austrian composer whose genius revealed itself with equal magnificence in his operas, symphonies, and instrumental works. He was born in Salzburg, January 27, 1756, and died in Vienna, December 5, 1791. His father, Leopold Mozart, a professional musician, guided Mozart's development as a child; he took him to Paris in 1763 and to England the following year. In both capitals, the child Mozart produced a profound impression, and a learned paper was published in England dealing with his astounding gifts. Mozart's early triumphs did not bring financial security, however, and he went to Vienna in search of employment. In the meantime, masterpieces of all descriptions continued to appear with miraculous spontaneity from his inexhaustible imagination. It is a common cliché to describe Mozart as a happy genius, a Raphael of music who willingly gave to the world an abundance of beauty incarnated in musical sounds. Indeed, it would be difficult to imagine, from the evidence of his music, that Mozart had great difficulties in making a living. However, letters addressed by Mozart to a friendly banker, asking for small loans of money, are extant; one such letter was recently sold at an autograph auction for a sum hundreds of times larger than the one originally requested by Mozart. After Mozart's death at the age of thirty-five, apparently of a kidney infection, melodramatic stories began to circulate accusing the respectable Italian musician Salieri of poisoning Mozart out of jealousy, a tale with no substance. Another tale, about a blinding snowstorm at Mozart's funeral, was disproved by the evidence obtained from the registries of the Vienna Weather Bureau. The greatness of Mozart's music lies in its inherent simplicity and communicative power. Of his operas, the greatest are undoubtedly *Le Nozze di Figaro*, produced in Vienna on May 1, 1786, and *Don Giovanni*, produced in Prague, October 29, 1787, both to Italian libretti. His last opera, *Die Zauberflöte*, produced in Vienna on September 30, 1791, was written to a German text. Mozart's instrumental works include many symphonies, chamber music, concertos, and a great number of sonatas and smaller pieces for piano. A catalogue of Mozart's compositions was compiled by an Austrian botanist and mineralogist, Ludwig von Köchel; the letter K in Mozart's list of works stands for Köchel.

MUDARRA, Alonso, Spanish lutenist and composer. He was born about 1508 and died in Seville, April 1, 1580. Apart from lute music, Mudarra composed madrigals and romanzas.

MUIR, Alexander, Canadian song writer. He was born in Scotland in 1830 and died in Canada in 1906. He went to Canada as a youth and became a school teacher in Toronto. He composed his famous song *The Maple Leaf Forever*, inspired by the Canadian emblem, in 1867, for a patriotic song contest sponsored by the Caledonian Society of Montreal; it won the second prize of $50.

MUIR, Lewis F., American composer and pianist. He was born in 1884 and died in 1950. He was active mainly as a vaudeville pianist and wrote a number of ragtimes, among them *Waiting for the Robert E. Lee.*

MUSSORGSKY, Modeste, great Russian composer of the national School. He was born in Karevo, in the district of Pskov, March 21, 1839, and died in St. Petersburg, March 28, 1881. He took piano lessons with various teachers in St. Petersburg; also served briefly in the regiment of the Imperial Guard. A meeting with Cui and Balakirev gave him an impetus to study music seriously. He had grandiose ideas about the future of truly national Russian music and launched a slogan, "To the new shores." Mussorgsky's name is associated with those of Rimsky-Korsakov, Balakirev, Borodin, and Cui as the "Mighty Five." The significance of Mussorgsky's genius was not realized in Russia until some time after his death. Rimsky-Korsakov undertook the necessary task of arranging and reorchestrating Mussorgsky's orchestral works, and virtually rewrote his operas *Boris Godunov* and *Khovanshchina*, as well as his *Songs and Dances of Death*. Mussorgsky's series of musical tableaux for piano, entitled *Pictures at an Exhibition*, which he wrote to illustrate in music the paintings of a friend, the Russian artist Victor Hartmann, is a Russian counterpart of Schumann's *Carnaval.*

NEUSIEDLER, Hans, German musician (his name is also spelled Newsidler). He was born in Pressburg, in 1508, and died in Nuremberg, February 2, 1563. He was a lutenist and published a number of pieces for the lute, mostly German dances.

NEWTON, Eddie, an American popular musician credited with the composition of the tune of the railroad ballad *Casey Jones*, which was inspired by an incident that occurred on April 29, 1900, when John Luther "Casey" Jones, an engineer for the Illinois Central Railroad, saw that his train "Cannon Ball Express" was going to ram a stalled freight train, and shouted to everyone to jump, but who himself remained at the controls of the engine and was killed. The composer, being a vaudeville performer, popularized the song himself. The words are by T. Lawrence Seibert. The song was published in 1909, in Los Angeles.

NICOLAI, Philipp, German cleric and hymn writer. He was born in Mengeringshausen, August 10, 1556, and died in Hamburg, October 26, 1608. He was the principal pastor at the St. Catherine church in Hamburg, and wrote words and melodies for many anthems, among them *Wachet auf, ruft uns die Stimme.*

NIELSEN, Carl, one of the most important Scandinavian composers of modern times. He was born in Nörre-Lyndelse, Denmark, June 9, 1865, and died in Copenhagen, October 3, 1931. He was a violinist and for many years played in various orchestras in Copenhagen. Eventually he became the conductor of the Royal Opera and president of the Royal Conservatory. A Romantic in his musical esthetics, Nielsen attached descriptive titles to his symphonies, such as *Sinfonia espansiva* and *The Inextinguishable*. He introduced bold innovations, especially in his harmonies, while preserving the tonal structure of his music even in his most modernistically designed scores.

NORTON, Caroline Elizabeth Sarah, English song writer. She was born in London in 1808 and died there in 1877. She is known mainly for her song *Juanita*, which she arranged from Handel's *Sarabande* in his opera *Almira* (1705). The same tune appears in Handel's aria *Lascia ch'io pianga* (*Let Me Cry*) from his opera *Rinaldo*, first produced in London in 1711. Mrs. Norton published the melody with her words in 1853, in her collection *Songs of Affection.*

OGIWARA, Toshitsugu, Japanese composer (also spelled Oghihara). He was born in Osaka, June 6, 1911. He was a student of Alexander Tcherepnin while the latter was in Tokyo. Ogiwara wrote a number of dance suites based on Japanese modes and many pieces of chamber music.

OLSEN, Ole, Norwegian composer. He was born in Hammerfest, July 4, 1850, and died in Oslo, November 10, 1927. He served as an organist and theater conductor in various Norwegian towns before going to Leipzig for regular music study. Returning to Norway, he was active as a teacher. He wrote several operas, symphonic works, and serenades for various instrumental ensembles.

PACHELBEL, Johann, German organist and composer. He was born in Nuremberg, September 1, 1653, and died there, March 3, 1706. He served as organist at St. Stephen's Cathedral in Vienna and was subsequently organist in various churches in Germany before returning to his native Nuremberg. His compositions for organ are regarded as fine examples of Baroque music. He wrote a *Chaconne* with thirteen variations, many fugues, and numerous other contrapuntal pieces.

PADEREWSKI, Ignace Jan, great Polish pianist, composer, and statesman. He was born in Kurylówka in Russian Poland, November 18, 1860, and died in New York, June 29, 1941. He studied piano at the Warsaw Conservatory and composition in Berlin. He subsequently went to Vienna for additional study with Leschetizky. He then began a career as pianist on a worldwide scale, with ever-increasing success, evoking unbounded adulation on the part of audiences and critics in Europe and the United States. He also made triumphant tours in South America, South Africa, and Australia. Paderewski was a Polish patriot, and during World War I he gave the proceeds from his concerts to Polish refugees. In 1919 he became Prime Minister of the newly formed Republic of Poland, but in the following year abandoned politics and resumed his pianistic career. After the invasion of Poland during World War II, Paderewski went to the United States and remained there until his death. Paderewski's only opera, *Manru,* was produced at the Metropolitan Opera in New York on February 14, 1902, and his symphony was first played in Boston, February 12, 1909. Neither work showed particular originality, but his unassuming piano piece *Menuet à l'antique* (known also as *Minuet in G*), which he wrote in 1887, became a universal favorite. Also popular are Paderewski's *Polish Dances* for piano, extracted from his *Tatra Album.*

PALMGREN, Selim, Finnish composer. He was born in Björneborg, February 16, 1878, and died in Helsinki, December 13, 1951. He studied at the Conservatory of Helsinki; later went to Berlin where he took piano lessons with Busoni. Returning to Finland, he was active as conductor and teacher. From 1923 to 1926 he was professor of composition at the Eastman School of Music in Rochester. He wrote two operas, five piano concertos, three symphonic poems, choral works, and a number of piano pieces of which *May Night* is the most popular.

PARKS, Henry Francis, American composer of popular songs. His arrangement of *Sucking Cider Through a Straw* is often performed.

PAUMANN, Conrad, celebrated German organist. He was born in Nuremberg, October 23, 1409, and died in Munich, January 24, 1473. He was blind from birth, but learned to play the organ, the harp, the lute, and the flute. In 1452 he published the oldest known organ manual, entitled *Fundamentum Organisandi.* It contains exercises and original compositions.

PERRY, Julia, American composer. She was born in Lexington, Kentucky, March 25, 1924. She studied at the Westminster Choir College (M.M., 1948). In 1952 she went to Italy and France and took private courses with Luigi Dallapiccola and Nadia Boulanger. An exceptionally prolific composer, she wrote two operas, *The Cask of Amontillado,* which was produced at Columbia University, November 20, 1954, and *The Selfish Giant.* From 1959 to 1972 she composed eleven symphonies. She also wrote a violin concerto and much chamber music and made orchestral transcriptions of Negro folksongs.

PESTALOZZA, Alberto, Italian composer. He was born in 1851 and died in 1934. In 1899 he published his most celebrated song, *Ciribiribin,* in waltz time. The front cover showed a couple kissing.

PHILE, Philip, German-American musician. He was born in Germany in 1734 and died in Philadelphia in 1793. He went to America and participated in the Revolutionary War. There are strong indications that he was the composer of *The President's March,* for which Joseph Hopkinson wrote the words *Hail, Columbia.*

PHILLIPS, Burrill, American composer and teacher. He was born in Omaha, Nebraska, November 9, 1907. He studied at the Eastman School of Music in Rochester with Bernard Rogers and Howard Hanson, and was on its faculty from 1933 to 1949. He subsequently taught at the University of Illinois (1949–1964). A prolific composer, he has written music for orchestra, chamber music, and effective teaching pieces for piano.

PIERPONT, John, American composer. He was born in Boston in 1822 and died in Winter Haven, Florida, in 1893. In 1857 he published a song under the title *One Horse Open Sleigh,* which was later published under a new title, *Jingle Bells,* whereupon it became celebrated as a Christmas song.

POLDINI, Eduard, Hungarian composer. He was born in Budapest, June 13, 1869, and died in Vevey, Switzerland, June 29, 1957. He studied piano and theory at the Budapest Conservatory and in 1908 settled in Switzerland. He wrote three operas and a great number of piano pieces of which *Poupée valsante,* written in 1895, is the most popular.

PRICE, Florence B., American pianist, composer, and educator. She was born in Little Rock, Arkansas, April 9, 1888, and died in Chicago, June 3, 1953. She studied at the New England Conservatory in Boston with Chadwick and Converse. Her works include a piano concerto, a violin concerto, and much chamber music, but she is known principally for her arrangements of Negro spirituals.

PROCTER, Alice McElroy, American pianist. She was born in Albany, New York, April 18, 1915. She studied at Smith College with Ross Lee Finney and Werner Josten (M.M., 1936), and later with Howard Hanson and Bernard Rogers at the Eastman School of Music in Rochester, where she received her Ph.D. She taught piano at various colleges, opened a piano studio in Milton, Massachusetts, in 1946, and published a number of teaching pieces for piano solo (*Footsteps in the Night, The Jumping Cat,* etc.), as well as works for two pianos. She is the wife of Leland H. Procter.

PROCTER, Leland H., American composer and teacher. He was born in Newton, Massachusetts, March 24, 1914. He studied theory at the Eastman School of Music in Rochester with Howard Hanson and Bernard Rogers (B.M., 1938) and at the University of Oklahoma (M.M.,

1940). He subsequently taught at the New England Conservatory in Boston (1946–1958). He was also active as mechanical designer and draftsman for various engineering concerns. Procter has written symphonic and chamber music and published teaching pieces for piano. He is the husband of the pianist Alice McElroy Procter.

PROKOFIEV, Sergei, one of the greatest modern composers of Russia. He was born in Sontzovka, near Ekaterinoslav, April 23, 1891, and died in Moscow, March 5, 1953. He studied composition with Glière in Moscow and then at the St. Petersburg Conservatory with Liadov and Rimsky-Korsakov. Prokofiev graduated in 1914 and was awarded first prize for his piano concerto which he performed at the commencement. Breaking away from traditional Russian Romanticism, he developed a style of composition animated by kinetic energy and marked by explosive rhythms. At the same time, he achieved a profound lyric expressiveness of the melodic line. In his early works he affected strong dissonant harmonies, but later he avoided strident combinations of sounds. To prove to himself and to others that he could handle the Classical techniques also, he wrote his *Classical Symphony* (1917) which became one of his most popular works. He left Russia after the Revolution and reached the United States by way of Siberia and the Orient. In America he gave piano recitals of his own works. Later he lived mostly in Paris. In 1933 he returned to Russia and resumed his Soviet citizenship. In 1936 he wrote his musical fairy tale *Peter and the Wolf*, which became a universal favorite. Among Prokofiev's operas, *The Love for Three Oranges*, first produced in Chicago in 1921, contains the celebrated march. Prokofiev wrote seven symphonies, a number of ballets among which *Romeo and Juliet* (1936) is best known, a great number of piano works, and songs. His piano suite *Visions Fugitives* exemplifies Prokofiev's lyrical humor. His *Toccata* for piano illustrates his percussive manner of writing for the instrument.

PUCCINI, Giacomo, famous Italian opera composer. He was born in Lucca, December 22, 1858, and died in Brussels, November 29, 1924. He studied in his home town and was a church organist before entering the Milan Conservatory where he studied composition with Ponchielli. He achieved his first success as an opera composer with the production in Turin of *Manon Lescaut* in 1893, which was followed three years later by his operatic masterpiece, *La Bohème*, to a libretto focused on the life of Bohemian artists in Paris. *La Bohème* was a historical landmark in the development of 'Verismo,' or theatrical realism. Puccini's later operas *Tosca* (1900) and *Madama Butterfly* (1904) established his reputation. His last opera was *Turandot*, which he had no time to complete. A niche by itself in Puccini's creative output belongs to *La Fanciulla del West (The Girl of the Golden West)*, written for America and produced at the Metropolitan Opera House in New York in 1910. In his technical idiom, Puccini made a decisive advance in the direction of modernism by introducing novel harmonic procedures and expanding the coloristic spectrum of melodic and rhythmic lines.

PURCELL, Henry, the greatest English composer of the seventeenth century. He was born about 1659 and died in Westminster, November 21, 1695. He served as a chorister at the Chapel Royal where he received instruction from John Blow, whom he succeeded as organist in 1679. His stated ambition was to emulate the art of the Italian song. However, he accomplished more than that and soon established himself as the creator of a national British genre of composition. His opera *Dido and Aeneas*, produced in 1689, was his masterpiece. Purcell wrote many ballads and songs in the English manner. The tablet at his tomb in Westminster Abbey epitomizes his contribution in the following words: "Here lyes Henry Purcell, Esq.; who left this life, and is gone to that blessed place where only his harmony can be exceeded."

RACHMANINOFF, Sergei, great Russian pianist and composer. He was born at Oneg, district of Novgorod, April 1, 1873, and died in Beverly Hills, California, March 28, 1943. He studied first with his cousin, the pianist and conductor Alexander Siloti, and then went to Moscow where he was a pupil of Taneyev and Arensky. His inspiration was derived from the Russian world of poetic melancholy associated with the music of Tchaikovsky. At the age of nineteen, Rachmaninoff wrote his *Prelude in C-sharp Minor*, a sonorous pianistic edifice, notated in the coda on four staves, which became one of the most celebrated single compositions for piano. Upon graduation from the Moscow Conservatory, Rachmaninoff undertook a concert tour in Russia, gradually acquiring fame as one of the greatest piano virtuosos of modern times. He continued to compose industriously and, at the age of twenty-eight, performed his *Second Piano Concerto* which became a standard piece in the piano repertory the world over. He made his first American tour in 1909. Returning to Russia, he continued his career as pianist and composer, but also conducted the Moscow Philharmonic Society. After the Revolution, Rachmaninoff left Russia, never to return. In 1935 he made his home in America, obtaining American citizenship shortly before his death. His *Rhapsody on a Theme by Paganini*, composed in 1934, became extremely popular. His songs, mostly to Russian texts, are marked by characteristic nostalgia without lapsing into sentimentality.

RAFF, Joachim, German composer. He was born in Lachen, near Zürich, Switzerland, May 27, 1822, and died in Frankfurt, June 25, 1882. After several years as a school teacher in Germany, he decided to devote himself to composition. One of the most prolific composers of the nineteenth century, Raff wrote eleven symphonies, several piano concertos, chamber music, choral works, and operas. His piano pieces achieved a certain vogue, but after his death their popularity declined.

RAMEAU, Jean-Philippe, one of the greatest masters of the French Baroque period. He was born in Dijon, September 25, 1683, and died in Paris, September 12, 1764.

He went to Italy as a youth to study music. Returning to France, he occupied various posts as church organist. In 1722 he published in Paris his fundamental work of music theory, *Traité de l'Harmonie*, which codified traditional usages. Rameau wrote a series of dramatic works and ballets for the Paris Opéra and participated in the polemical exchange in the 1750's with the adherents of the Italian dramatic methods, an episode known as *La Guerre des Bouffons*. His keyboard pieces achieved great popularity; perhaps the most famous of them is *Le Tambourin* which imitates the rhythmic beat of the "gypsy" drum.

RAVEL, Maurice, one of the most significant French composers of the modern era. He was born in Ciboure, March 7, 1875, and died in Paris, December 28, 1937. He was brought to Paris as a child and studied composition at the Paris Conservatory with Gabriel Fauré whose influence on Ravel's style was decisive. The well-known *Pavane pour une Infante défunte*, composed in 1899, reflects this influence in its characteristic modal structure. Ravel's piano piece *Jeux d'eau* (1902) epitomizes the novel type of French piano writing. His power to evoke the Classical and Romantic styles in a modern manner is revealed in *Le Tombeau de Couperin* for piano and *La Valse* for orchestra. His ballet score *Boléro* is a perennial favorite.

REBIKOV, Vladimir, Russian composer of the modern school. He was born in Krasnoyarsk, Siberia, May 31, 1866, and died in Yalta, August 4, 1920. He studied at the Moscow Conservatory, then travelled to Berlin and Vienna for further lessons in composition. Returning to Russia, he lived in Moscow. After the Revolution he moved to the Crimea where he died. He emulated Impressionistic usages in his piano pieces and introduced a novel genre of rhythmic declamations for voice and piano. His opera *The Christmas Tree* contains a popular waltz; he also wrote some characteristic pieces and dances for piano solo.

REDFORD, John, English organist and composer. He lived in the first half of the sixteenth century and died in London in 1547.

REDNER, Lewis H., American organist and hymn composer. He was born in Philadelphia in 1831 and died in Atlantic City in 1908. He served as church organist in Philadelphia and was also active as Sunday School superintendent. In 1874 he wrote the music for the hymn *O Little Town of Bethlehem* to the words of Phillips Brooks, and the setting became a standard in the church repertory.

REICHARDT, Johannes Friedrich, German composer of chamber music and songs. He was born in Königsberg, November 25, 1752, and died in Giebichenstein, near Halle, June 27, 1814. He studied music and philosophy in Königsberg and Leipzig. In 1775 he was appointed court composer to Frederick the Great. He later lived in Kassel and in Halle. A prolific composer, he wrote symphonies, sonatas, trios, and quartets. He is renowned for his songs and anthems.

REINECKE, Carl, German pianist and composer. He was born in Altona, June 23, 1824, and died in Leipzig, March 10, 1910. After learning the rudiments of music from his father, a professional musician, he went to Leipzig where he met Mendelssohn and Schumann. He travelled as a concert pianist in Germany and Denmark, held various teaching posts, and in 1860 was appointed conductor of the Gewandhaus Concerts in Leipzig. He also was professor of piano and composition at the Leipzig Conservatory. His characteristic pieces for piano enjoy a certain vogue. He is also renowned for his brilliant cadenzas to piano concertos of Mozart and Beethoven.

RESPIGHI, Ottorino, Italian composer of the Modern School. He was born in Bologna, July 9, 1879, and died in Rome, April 18, 1936. After studying composition in Italy, he went to Russia where he took lessons with Rimsky-Korsakov. For many years he was also active as an orchestral violinist. In 1913 he was appointed professor of composition at the Santa Cecilia School in Rome. He toured the United States in 1925 and in 1932 as conductor and pianist. He wrote several operas, but achieved fame through his symphonic poems *Fontane di Roma* and *I Pini di Roma*, brilliant evocations of Roman scenes.

RICE, Thomas N., American pianist and composer. He was born in Washington, D.C., February 6, 1933. He attended the Catholic University in Washington and the University of North Carolina. His teaching pieces for piano include *I Mean It!*, *Shifting*, and *Two-Keys Etude*. He also wrote orchestral and chamber music.

RIMSKY-KORSAKOV, Nikolai, great Russian composer. He was born in Tikhvin, near Novgorod, March 18, 1844, and died in Liubensk, near St. Petersburg, June 21, 1908. In 1856 he entered the Naval Academy and in 1862 went on a sea voyage on the clipper Almaz which made stops in the United States during the Civil War, and in Brazil. Rimsky-Korsakov received fundamental training from Balakirev and acquired sufficient technique to compose a symphony which Balakirev conducted in St. Petersburg on December 31, 1865. It was the first symphony written by a Russian composer. An association with Borodin, Cui, Mussorgsky, and Balakirev led to the formation of a group later known as the "Mighty Five," whose proclaimed purpose was to promote authentic Russian music independent of foreign influences. Rimsky-Korsakov's prime accomplishment is in the field of Russian opera; almost all his librettos are based on Russian subjects of history or legend. He was a master of colorful instrumentation. His symphonic suite *Scheherazade* is a brilliant evocation of Oriental scenes. His songs are notable for the important role he gave to the piano accompaniment. He also was an eminent educator; among his students were Glazunov, Liadov, Stravinsky, and Prokofiev. As editor for the Belaieff publishing house he gave great impetus to the publication of music by a number of Russian composers.

ROOT, George F., American composer of popular ballads. He was born in Sheffield, Massachusetts, August 30, 1820, and died on Bailey's Island, Maine, August 6, 1895. He was church organist in New York and later moved to Chicago where he joined a publishing firm. His song *The Battle Cry of Freedom* has achieved great popularity.

ROSEINGRAVE, Thomas, English organist. He was born in Winchester, 1690, and died in Dunleary, June 23, 1766. He studied with his father. In 1710 he travelled to Italy where he met Domenico Scarlatti. The *Allemande* from his organ suite in G minor bears the subtitle *Introduction to Scarlatti.*

ROSS, Alexander Coffman, American composer of popular songs. He was born in 1812 and died in 1883. His fame rests exclusively on his campaign song *Tippecanoe and Tyler Too,* which he wrote in 1840 for the election of William Henry Harrison as President and John Tyler as Vice President. Tippecanoe was a nickname Harrison got for his victory over the Indians in Tippecanoe, Indiana, in 1811. Harrison died of pneumonia a month after taking office, whereupon John Tyler became President.

ROSSI, Padre Michel Angelo, Italian composer. He was born in Rome in 1600 and died in 1674. He studied with Frescobaldi in Rome, then served as organist and court composer in Italy. He published a collection of organ pieces in a traditional Baroque style.

ROUGET de l'Isle. See **LISLE.**

RUBINSTEIN, Anton, great Russian pianist and composer. He was born in Vykhvatinetz, November 28, 1829, and died in Peterhof, near St. Petersburg, November 20, 1894. He was a member of a Jewish merchant family, but was baptized as an infant. This enabled the family to move to Moscow where unbaptized Jews were not allowed to reside. He studied piano with Alexandre Villoing. So extraordinary was his progress that he was engaged as a youth for a concert tour of Europe. Returning to Russia, Rubinstein began to compose industriously. He wrote his famous *Melody in F* at the age of twenty-three, while staying at the palace of the Grand Duchess Helen on Kamennoi-Ostrow (Stone Island), an aristocratic suburb of St. Petersburg. Two years later he published an *Album de Portraits pour piano* containing twenty-four pieces, including one named *Kamennoi-Ostrow,* which also became very popular. His early *Ocean Symphony* was highly successful and was praised by Liszt. Rubinstein was also active as an educator. In 1862 he founded the Imperial Conservatory in St. Petersburg and was its director until 1867. In 1872 he embarked on an extensive American tour; his playing entirely from memory, a novel practice at the time, was hailed in the American press as an extraordinary achievement.

SAINT-AMANS, Louis, French song composer. He was born in 1749 and died in 1820. His *Tricotet,* subtitled *Ninette at Court,* has enjoyed a certain popularity.

SAINT-SAËNS, Camille, celebrated French composer. He was born in Paris, October 9, 1835, and died in Algiers, December 16, 1921. He was a child prodigy. He studied piano and organ at the Paris Conservatory and, upon graduation, became a church organist. He was praised by Liszt and Wagner as pianist and composer. His opera *Samson et Dalila* (1877) has become a repertory piece all over the world. His *Third Symphony* (1886), with its important organ part, is widely performed. Also popular are his piano concertos. His instrumental suite *Le Carnaval des Animaux* is a fine example of representational animal music; one movement, *Le Cygne,* for cello solo, was immortalized by Anna Pavlova in a ballet tableau of a dying swan. His *Danse Macabre,* which exists in numerous arrangements, is also extremely popular.

SCARLATTI, Alessandro, Italian composer of operas and oratorios, and renowned founder of the Neapolitan School of music. He was born in Palermo, May 2, 1660, and died in Naples, October 24, 1725. He went to Rome as a child. At one time he was attached to the court of Queen Christina of Sweden, then resident in Rome. In 1709 he settled in Naples. His principal achievement was to establish the form of the da capo aria (in which the first section is repeated) and the accompanied recitative. Both devices are associated with the rise of the Neapolitan School.

SCARLATTI, Domenico, famous Italian composer of keyboard music, son of Alessandro Scarlatti. He was born in Naples, October 26, 1685, and died in Madrid, July 23, 1757. He received his early musical education from his father, and was engaged as organist at the age of sixteen. After holding various posts in Rome, he was appointed organist at the Vatican in 1714. In 1729 he went to Madrid as court musician. He is rightly regarded as the founder of the modern technique of keyboard playing, a technique requiring advanced digital dexterity, including crossing of the hands. One of his fugues, which has a theme of wide intervallic leaps, is popularly known as the *Cat's Fugue,* purportedly suggested to Scarlatti by his cat's walk over the keyboard.

SCHARWENKA, Philipp, German composer and educator. He was born in Samter, Posen, February 16, 1847, and died in Bad Nauheim, July 16, 1917. He studied at Kullak's Academy in Berlin, where he later became a teacher. In 1881 he organized the Scharwenka Conservatory in Berlin with his brother Xaver Scharwenka. He was highly regarded as a pedagogue. Many of his characteristically romantic piano pieces have become popular.

SCHOENBERG, Arnold, great Austrian composer and innovator, creator of the method of composition with twelve tones. He was born in Vienna, September 13, 1874, and died in Los Angeles, July 13, 1951. His early works belong to the Wagnerian tradition. He then gradually veered away from established tonality, abandoned the key signature, and evolved a distinct Expressionistic idiom. His *Piano Pieces Opus 19* are representative of this new style. In 1912 he produced his revolutionary song cycle *Pierrot Lunaire*, in which he made use of *Sprechgesang* (speech-song). About 1924 he formulated the basic laws of twelve-tone technique, in which the principal theme consists of twelve different chromatic tones, and the same theme, or "tone row," forms the foundation of the harmony. In Schoenberg's music, dissonances are emancipated, but traditional formal elements remain very strong. In 1933 Schoenberg left Germany, where he had been teaching for many years, and sought refuge in America, eventually settling in Los Angeles. Some of his most important works, among them the violin concerto, piano concerto, and the cantata *A Survivor from Warsaw*, were composed in America. Among Schoenberg's most notable early disciples are Alban Berg, Anton Webern, and Ernst Krenek. The influence of the twelve-tone method is worldwide: virtually all composers of the twentieth century have made use of it, including Stravinsky in the last years of his creative life.

SCHUBERT, Franz, great Austrian composer, creator of the Romantic form of the art song, or Lied. He was born in Vienna, January 31, 1797, and died there, November 19, 1828. He was a pupil of Salieri. His facility was magical; by the time he was eighteen he had written as many as 150 songs, including such masterpieces as *Erlkönig* and *Die Forelle*. In these songs he perfected what has become known as the German Lied. He applied a similar approach to his piano compositions, particularly his *Impromptus* and *Moments Musicaux*. His symphonies reflect the true romantic spirit of his time. His overtures and ballets are equally inspired. His chamber music demonstrates, in addition, a remarkable mastery of contrapuntal techniques. Only a few works were published in his lifetime; his famous *Unfinished Symphony* was not discovered until forty years after his death.

SCHUMANN, Robert, great German composer. He was born in Zwickau, June 8, 1810, and died in Endenich, near Bonn, July 29, 1856. He studied law and philosophy at the University of Leipzig, and later began to take piano lessons with Friedrich Wieck, the father of Clara Wieck whom he eventually married. Fascinated by literary Romanticism, Schumann composed characteristic pieces for piano with descriptive titles. Thus his celebrated *Carnaval* for piano is based on a group of notes spelling out the name of the town of Asch in German notation (*As* being A-flat, and, in another variant, S being *Es*, for E-flat). Fantasy dominated his imagination. In 1834 Schumann founded the journal *Neue Zeitschrift für Musik*, which became the organ of the Romantic School. In 1843 he was invited by Mendelssohn to teach at the Leipzig Conservatory. Later he lived in Dresden, and in 1850 he became town musical director in Düsseldorf. By that time the symptoms of his mental illness, first revealed when Schumann was a youth, became acute. Schumann tried to drown himself in the Rhine, but was saved. He was then taken to an asylum where he died without recovering full possession of his faculties. As a master of the Lied, Schumann approached the heights of Schubert. His piano concerto and other piano music are gems of the Romantic literature. His four symphonies occupy an important place in orchestral music.

SCHÜTT, Eduard, pianist and composer. He was born in St. Petersburg, Russia, October 22, 1856, and died in Obermias, near Merano, Italy, July 26, 1933. He studied at the St. Petersburg Conservatory and later at the Leipzig Conservatory, then became a piano student of Leschetizky in Vienna where he eventually settled. As a composer, he is chiefly remembered for his effective piano pieces.

SCHYTTE, Ludvig, Danish composer. He was born in Aarhus, April 28, 1848, and died in Berlin, November 10, 1909. He studied composition with Niels V. Gade, and later was a piano pupil of Liszt in Weimar. He lived in Vienna for some twenty years as a piano teacher. During the last years of his life he taught in Berlin. Schytte wrote principally for piano; his pieces are couched in an effective, Romantic style. He also published some piano studies.

SCOTT, Lady John (Alicia Anne Spottiswoode), Scottish amateur composer who wrote the famous song *Annie Laurie*. She was born in Spottiswoode, Scotland, in 1810, and died there in 1900 at the age of ninety. She wrote *Annie Laurie* in 1835. It seems that Annie Laurie was a real person. The words of the song are attributed to the Scottish swain William Douglas who was in love with Annie Laurie, but since he belonged to a rival Scottish clan, she married another. *Annie Laurie* became popular among British soldiers during the Crimean War, and it retained its sentimental appeal well into the twentieth century.

SCRIABIN, Alexander, great Russian composer and innovator. He was born in Moscow, January 6, 1872, and died there, April 27, 1915. He studied piano at the Moscow Conservatory with Safonov and composition with Arensky. His early compositions are in the manner of Chopin; very soon, however, Scriabin evolved his own unmistakable style. He increased the spectrum of piano technique, eventually outgrowing the framework of traditional forms. The ethereal harmonies which he cultivated led to a completely free use of dissonant combinations. His last symphonic poem, *Prometheus*, derives its entire thematic material from a "mystic chord" consisting of six notes (C, F-sharp, B-flat, E, A, D). Scriabin introduced in the score of *Prometheus* a special part for a "color keyboard," but experiments with such a device have been largely unsuccessful. The titles of his works—*Divine Poem, Poem of Ecstasy, Poème satanique, Vers la flamme*—indicate Scriabin's leanings towards mysticism.

SEEGER, Charles, American music scholar and composer. He was born of American parents in Mexico City, December 14, 1886. He graduated from Harvard University in 1908, and was on the faculty of the University of California, Los Angeles, from 1912 to 1919 and again from 1950 to 1970. He was a founder of the American Musicological Society in 1934. He composed overtures, pageants, and some chamber music. With his wife, Ruth

Crawford (1901–1953), an adventurous composer in her own right, he did valuable research work in American folk music.

SEIXAS, Carlos, Portuguese composer. He was born in Coimbra, June 11, 1704, and died in Lisbon, August 25, 1742. He studied organ and served as church organist in Lisbon. His keyboard works are fine examples of Baroque writing.

SHEPHERD, Arthur, American composer and educator. He was born in Paris, Idaho, February 19, 1880, and died in Cleveland, January 12, 1958. He studied at the New England Conservatory in Boston with Goetschius and Chadwick. From 1897 to 1908 he was active in Salt Lake City. Returning to Boston, he taught at the New England Conservatory. From 1920 to 1926 he was assistant conductor of the Cleveland Orchestra, and from 1927 to 1950 he taught music at Western Reserve University. In his works he cultivated American themes; some of his songs and piano pieces are written in an exotic manner.

SHOSTAKOVICH, Dmitri, the most significant Soviet composer after Prokofiev. He was born in St. Petersburg, September 25, 1906. He studied at the St. Petersburg Conservatory, graduating in piano and composition. His *First Symphony,* which he wrote as a graduation piece at the age of eighteen, produced a striking impression by its novelty and kinetic energy. Performed abroad, it became Shostakovich's most popular orchestral work. Of his other symphonies, the *Seventh,* known as the "Leningrad Symphony" because it was partly composed during the siege of Leningrad, enjoyed great popularity during and immediately after World War II. In 1970 he wrote his fifteenth symphony. His other works include thirteen string quartets, two violin concertos, two piano concertos, and two cello concertos, an opera *Lady Macbeth of the District of Mtzensk,* ballets, and film music. On his sixtieth birthday, in 1966, Shostakovich was awarded the Order of Hero of Socialist Labor.

SIBELIUS, Jean, great Finnish composer. He was born in Tavastehus, December 8, 1865, and died in Järvenpää, September 20, 1957. He studied violin and composition at the Helsingfors Conservatory and theory in Berlin and Vienna. From his first steps in composition, he was determined to express the essence of Finnish folksongs in European Classical and Romantic forms. In this he brilliantly succeeded. With the national epic poem *Kalevala* as his principal source of inspiration, he wrote a symphonic poem *Kullervo,* which was followed by *En Saga* and *The Swan of Tuonela.* In 1900 he produced his celebrated orchestral work *Finlandia,* which became a musical symbol of Finnish nationalism. Sibelius wrote seven symphonies, a violin concerto, and many short pieces for violin. His *Valse Triste* is very popular and is available in numerous arrangements; originally it was a part of the incidental music to the Finnish drama *Kuolema,* performed in 1903.

SIFLER, Paul J., Austrian-American pianist. He was born in Austria in 1921. He came to the United States as a child. He studied music with Leo Sowerby at the American Conservatory in Chicago, then continued his studies at Westminster Choir College in Princeton, New Jersey. Sifler wrote for voice, for organ, and for piano. Among his teaching pieces are *A Humming Tune, Tolling Bells,* and *The Ugly Duckling.*

SILCHER, Friedrich, German song composer. He was born in Schnaith, Württemberg, June 27, 1789, and died in Tübingen, August 26, 1860. He was active mainly as a choral conductor and published several collections of German folksongs. He achieved fame through his song *Lorelei* to words by Heinrich Heine.

SINDING, Christian, Norwegian composer. He was born in Kongsberg, January 11, 1856, and died in Oslo, December 3, 1941. He studied at the Leipzig Conservatory and published most of his music in Germany. He visited America in 1921 at the invitation of George Eastman, and taught at the Eastman School of Music in Rochester. He then returned to Norway. He wrote operas, symphonies, and much chamber music, but he is remembered chiefly through his attractive piano piece *Rustles of Spring,* written in a Lisztian manner.

SMETANA, Bedřich, outstanding national Czech composer. He was born in Leitomischl, March 2, 1824, and died in Prague, May 12, 1884. He studied piano and composition at the Prague Conservatory, was active as a concert pianist and conductor but eventually concentrated on composition. After the indifferent success of his first opera, he wrote the comic music drama *The Bartered Bride* (1866), which became universally popular. In 1874 he created his symphonic masterpiece, *My Country,* a suite in six movements of which one, *The Moldau,* became an orchestral classic. During the last years of his life he was afflicted by almost total deafness. Finally, insanity also set in, and he had to be confined to an asylum where he died. Smetana is regarded as the founder, with Dvořák, of the Bohemian national School of composition. It is interesting to note that the Israeli national anthem, *Hatikvah,* is practically identical with the tune of *The Moldau.*

SMITH, John Stafford, English composer of hymns and anthems. He was born in Gloucester about 1750 and died in London, September 21, 1836. He was active as an organist. In 1785 he was appointed lay-vicar at Westminster Abbey. He published several collections of glees and catches, for which he won prizes given by the Catch Club of London. The fifth collection of glees, published in 1799, includes an arrangement of the song *To Anacreon in Heaven.* Francis Scott Key used this tune to write the patriotic poem *The Star-Spangled Banner* in 1814, while watching the bombardment by the British of Fort McHenry. Some American scholars and historians regard John Stafford Smith as the composer of the tune, but there is no supporting evidence.

SMITH, Julia, American pianist and composer. She was born in Denton, Texas, January 25, 1911. She studied piano with Carl Friedberg at the Institute of Musical Art in New York, and received her Ph.D. from New York University. Her teachers in composition were Rubin Goldmark and Frederick Jacobi. She composed symphonic and chamber music, a piano concerto, and other piano works. Her teaching pieces for piano include *Blue Nocturne, Comanche War, Dancing School,* and *Little Sputnik March.*

SOUSA, John Philip, famous American bandmaster and composer, renowned as "The March King." He was born in Washington, D.C., November 6, 1854, the son of a Portuguese father and a Bavarian mother, and died in Reading, Pennsylvania, March 6, 1932. He played in the Marine Band as a youth and in 1880 was appointed its conductor. In 1892 he organized a band of his own and toured with it in America and Europe with enormous success. His march *The Stars and Stripes Forever* achieved national stature as a patriotic tune. Among his other celebrated march tunes are *El Capitan, King Cotton,* and *The Liberty Bell.*

SOWERBY, Leo, American composer. He was born in Grand Rapids, Michigan, May 1, 1895, and died in Port Clinton, Ohio, July 7, 1968. He studied music in Chicago. In 1921 he was awarded the first American Prix de Rome to be given for composition. After three years in Rome he taught at the American Conservatory in Chicago. In 1962 he was appointed director of the College for Church Musicians at the National Cathedral in Washington, D.C. An exceptionally prolific composer, he wrote symphonic works, concertos, choruses, and chamber music, all in a fine, traditional manner, often with a touch of humor. His song *Lydia Pinkham* evokes the nostalgic era of American home remedies.

SPILMAN, Jonathan Edwards, American composer. He was born in Greenville, Kentucky, in 1812, and died in Flora, Illinois, in 1896. He was a lawyer and later a minister. In 1838 he published the song *Flow Gently, Sweet Afton,* to words of Robert Burns.

STAINER, Sir John, English organist and composer. He was born in London, June 6, 1840, and died in Verona, Italy, March 31, 1901. As a young boy, he was a chorister at St. Paul's Cathedral in London. In 1872 he was appointed organist there, resigning in 1888, the year when he was knighted. In 1889 he became professor of music at Oxford University. He wrote a number of oratorios, church services, anthems, and songs. His arrangement of the old sixteenth-century hymn *Good King Wenceslas* is often used in choral concerts.

STEENWICK, Gisbert, an English composer of hymns, who died in 1679. His anthem *Blessed Bethlehem* is often sung.

STEFFE, William. He was a Philadelphia man whose claim of the authorship of *The Battle Hymn of the Republic* has been supported by some. Other claimants are Thomas Brigham Bishop of New York, and Frank E. Jerome of Russell, Kansas. The song is also known under the titles *Glory Hallelujah,* and *John Brown's Body Lies a-Mouldering in the Grave.* (The John Brown of the song was a Sergeant at Fort Warren at Boston Harbor, not the famous crusader who led the raid on Harper's Ferry in 1859.) The music apparently originated with a vocal quartet of the Second Battalion of Massachusetts Infantry, known as "Tigers," of which John Brown was a member. Julia Ward Howe wrote the poem *Battle Hymn of the Republic* in 1862, and the words were adapted to the tune of *Glory Hallelujah,* which already was popular then.

STILL, William Grant, eminent American Negro composer. He was born in Woodville, Mississippi, May 11, 1895. He studied at Oberlin Conservatory and later with George W. Chadwick in Boston. He also took lessons with Edgard Varèse, from whom he received ideas for an advanced style of composition. He eventually settled in Los Angeles. Still has written four symphonies, several symphonic poems, six operas, three ballets, and many other works, virtually all inspired by American and African Negro elements. His *Afro-American Symphony* is a classic of its genre.

STÖLZEL, Gottfried Heinrich, German composer. He was born in Grünstädtel, January 13, 1690, and died in Gotha, November 27, 1749. He studied in Leipzig, then became a music teacher in Breslau where he produced his early operas. Later he travelled in Italy, was for a time in Prague and in Bayreuth, and finally settled in Gotha. He wrote twenty-two operas, fourteen oratorios, and much instrumental music in the traditional Baroque style.

STONE, Kurt, American musicologist and editor. He was born in Hamburg, Germany, November 14, 1911. He studied music in Hamburg and later in Copenhagen. In 1938 he settled in America where he entered the field of music publishing. He has held editorial positions with G. Schirmer, Inc., and other houses and was editor-in-chief of Associated Music Publishers, Inc., for many years. In 1968 he was appointed Project Coordinator for the New Scribner Music Library. An expert on modern music and critical analysis, Stone has contributed many important articles on contemporary music and its composers. He is director of the Index of New Musical Notation at the New York Public Library.—He has provided numerous accompaniments and realizations of continuo basses, etc., for the New Scribner Music Library. He has also contributed the Pictorial History of Keyboard Instruments in Volume 11 (Reference Volume).

STRATEGIER, Herman, Dutch composer. He was born in Arnhem, August 10, 1912. He was church organist in his home town and later moved to Utrecht. His compositions include chamber music and many songs; he also arranged Dutch dances for piano.

STRAUS, Oscar, Austrian composer of operettas. He was born in Vienna, March 6, 1870, and died in Ischl, January 11, 1954. He studied in Vienna with Grädener and in

Berlin with Max Bruch. At the outbreak of World War II, he went to America, returning to Austria in 1948. His most celebrated operetta is *Der tapfere Soldat* (1908), after G. B. Shaw, known in England and America under the title *The Chocolate Soldier*. Almost as popular was his operetta *Ein Walzertraum* (*A Waltz Dream*), produced in Vienna in 1907. The waltzes from it are often played.

STRAUSS, Johann, Jr., celebrated Austrian composer of waltzes, nicknamed "The Waltz King." He was born in Vienna, October 25, 1825, and died there, June 3, 1899. His father, Johann Strauss Sr., who initiated the vogue of the Viennese waltz and was in fact known as "The Father of the Waltz," opposed his son's ambition to become a musician, but Johann Jr. formed his own restaurant band and gradually became celebrated as bandleader and waltz composer in his own right. He wrote 498 opus numbers of dance music. His best known waltz is *The Blue Danube*, composed in 1867. Other celebrated waltz tunes by him are *Artist Life, Roses from the South, Tales from the Vienna Woods, Vienna Blood, Voices of Spring,* and *Wine, Women, and Song.* Far from being considered a plebeian type of music by his great contemporaries, the Strauss waltzes were admired by Brahms and Wagner, among others. Strauss also wrote numerous operettas of which *Die Fledermaus* is the most popular.

STRAUSS, Josef, Austrian composer of light music, brother of Johann Strauss, Jr. He was born in Vienna, August 22, 1827, and died there, July 21, 1870. Almost as prolific as his celebrated brother, he published 283 opus numbers. His *Pizzicato Polka* is extremely popular.

STRAUSS, Richard, great German composer, creator of a new type of philosophical symphonic poem. He was born in Munich, June 11, 1864, and died at Garmisch-Partenkirchen, September 8, 1949. He received his early musical education from his father, a famous French horn player, and began to compose as a young boy. His early works are set in a traditional manner, but beginning with the composition of the tone poem *Don Juan*, at the age of twenty-five, Strauss emerged as an innovator, transferring the Wagnerian system of leitmotivs into the symphonic field. Hans von Bülow described Strauss as "Richard the Second," thus bestowing on him Wagner's mantle. Virtually all great tone poems of Strauss were composed before he reached the age of thirty-five: *Death and Transfiguration* (1889), *Till Eulenspiegel* (1895), *Thus Spake Zarathustra* (1896), *Don Quixote* (1897), and *Ein Heldenleben* (1898). In the twentieth century Strauss turned to operas, producing the epoch-making *Salome* (1907) and *Elektra* (1909). As if to demonstrate his ability to please audiences, he wrote *Der Rosenkavalier* (1911), an ingratiating operatic score, replete with attractive waltz tunes. His songs of an early period are sung in concerts everywhere.

STRAVINSKY, Igor, great Russian composer. He was born in Oranienbaum, June 17, 1882, and died in New York, April 6, 1971. After harmony studies with Akimenko and Kalafati, Stravinsky took private lessons with Rimsky-Korsakov. His first important work was the ballet *The Firebird*, which he wrote for Diaghilev's Ballet Russe in Paris in 1910. His second ballet, also written for Diaghilev, was *Pétrouchka*, a tableau of the Russian fair. Here Stravinsky introduced harmonic and rhythmic innovations which became the hallmarks of his idiom. There followed the epoch-making score of *Le Sacre du printemps*, produced by Diaghilev in Paris in 1913. Its uncompromising use of dissonance and primitivistic rhythms shocked the Paris audience, but profoundly impressed the young generation of musicians. Stravinsky lived mostly in Switzerland and in France, returning to Russia for a brief visit in 1962 after forty-eight years abroad. He made his first American trip in 1925 and eventually settled in the United States and became an American citizen. As a composer, he changed his style about 1920, abandoning the Russian luxuriance of his early ballets in favor of a more austere, Neo-Classical idiom. Another significant change in Stravinsky's style supervened about 1950, when he began composing in a modified dodecaphonic (twelve-tone) idiom.

SULLIVAN, Sir Arthur, English composer of light opera. He was born in London, May 13, 1842, and died there, November 22, 1900. He studied music at the Royal Academy in London and later at the Leipzig Conservatory. In 1875 he formed an association with the writer of satirical verse W. S. Gilbert, and with him as the librettist produced a series of "Gilbert and Sullivan" comic operas that became enormously successful in England and America. Of these, the most famous are *H.M.S. Pinafore* (1878), *The Pirates of Penzance* (1879), and *The Mikado* (1885). Although Sullivan regarded himself primarily as a composer of serious works, his grand opera *Ivanhoe* (1891) failed to attain significant success. However, his religious hymn *Onward, Christian Soldiers*, composed in 1864, became a perennial favorite. Equally popular is his song *The Lost Chord*, written in 1877.

SWANDER, Don, American composer. He was born in Marshalltown, Iowa, in 1905. In 1941 he wrote the tune of the celebrated song *Deep in the Heart of Texas*, to the words of his wife, June Hershey (who had never been to Texas).

TALLIS, Thomas, English organist and composer. He was born about 1505 and died in Greenwich, November 23, 1585. He was attached to the Chapel Royal as organist and instructor during the reigns of Henry VIII, Edward VI, Queen Mary, and Queen Elizabeth. He was a master contrapuntist; his motets and anthems, both to Latin and English words, are comparable in excellence to those of his great contemporary, William Byrd. He also wrote some keyboard music.

TALMA, Louise, American composer. She was born in Arcachon, France, October 31, 1906. She attended New York University and Columbia University, then went to France where she studied piano with Isidore Philipp and composition with Nadia Boulanger. Returning to New York, she joined the staff of Hunter College. She has received many awards, among them two Guggenheim Grants. Her *Dialogues* for piano and orchestra received the Concerto Award in the Fifth International Competition for Women Composers in Mannheim, Germany. Her opera *The Alcestiad* was premiered in Frankfurt in 1962. She also wrote a *Toccata* for orchestra, the oratorio *The Divine Flame*, a piano sonata, choral works, and short pieces for various instruments.

TCHAIKOVSKY, Peter Ilyich, celebrated Russian composer. He was born in Votkinsk, district of Viatka, May 7, 1840, and died in St. Petersburg, November 6, 1893. His family moved to St. Petersburg when he was ten years old. He studied law before deciding on a musical career. He was a piano student of Anton Rubinstein in St. Petersburg. In 1866 he was engaged as harmony instructor at the Moscow Conservatory. Tchaikovsky began to compose rather late in life; his first important work, the overture-fantasy *Romeo and Juliet*, was composed in 1869. This was the beginning of an astoundingly fruitful quarter of a century of creative work. Tchaikovsky wrote eleven operas of which *Eugene Onegin* and *The Queen of Spades* are best known. He also wrote the ballets *Swan Lake, The Sleeping Beauty,* and *The Nutcracker,* six symphonies concluding with the *Pathétique,* the symphonic fantasy *Francesca da Rimini,* the orchestral *Italian Capriccio,* the *Serenade* for string orchestra, and the popular *1812 Overture.* His first piano concerto is the pièce de résistance for virtuoso pianists; his violin concerto is a standard repertory piece. Among his works of chamber music, the first string quartet and the piano trio are frequently played. His pieces for solo piano include the poetic *Barcarole* from his suite of twelve characteristic pieces, each named after a month of the year, and the nostalgic *Chanson Triste.* Tchaikovsky wrote more than one hundred songs, distinguished by an exquisite melodic line in a resonant harmonic setting. He was not a brilliant performer, either as pianist or conductor, but he had numerous engagements to conduct orchestras in Europe. In 1891 he also made a concert tour in America. His personal life was dramatic; he once attempted suicide. Fearful of cholera, which had taken his mother's life, he fell victim to an epidemic himself.

TCHEREPNIN, Alexander, Russian composer. He was born in St. Petersburg, January 20, 1899, a son of the eminent Russian composer and pedagogue Nicolas Tcherepnin. Encouraged by his father, he began to compose early in life. The Revolution disrupted his career: he travelled to the Caucasus, then went to Paris where he took piano lessons with Isidor Philipp and counterpoint with Paul Vidal. He toured widely. Between 1934 and 1937 he travelled to China and Japan, and married the Chinese pianist Lee Hsien-Ming. In 1938 he settled in Paris where he remained until 1947. In 1949 he went to the United States. A very prolific composer, Tcherepnin wrote operas, symphonies, ballets, concertos, and much chamber music. In a majority of his works he applies a scale of nine notes, which lends itself to exotic combinations of sounds. His piano pieces are marked by

great virtuosity and imaginative use of technical resources.

TELEMANN, Georg Philipp, a significant German composer, contemporary of Bach and Handel. He was born in Magdeburg, March 14, 1681, and died in Hamburg, June 25, 1767. He studied law at Leipzig University and also organized a choral society. In 1721 he moved to Hamburg. Telemann wrote some forty operas, a great number of sacred works, and much chamber music. His keyboard compositions exhibit consummate contrapuntal skill.

THOMÉ, Francis, French composer. He was born in Port Louis, on the island of Mauritius, October 18, 1850, and died in Paris, November 16, 1909. He settled in Paris as a young man and studied piano and composition at the Paris Conservatory. He wrote several operas and ballets. His piano pieces *Simple Aveu* and *Sous la Feuillée* are favorites with piano teachers and music lovers.

THOMSON, Virgil, outstanding American composer, creator of a unique style of sophisticated simplicity. He was born in Kansas City, Missouri, November 25, 1896. He studied piano with Heinrich Gebhard and organ with Wallace Goodrich in Boston. Later he took lessons in composition with Rosario Scalero in New York and Nadia Boulanger in Paris. He was graduated from Harvard University in 1922. In 1925 he went to Paris where he met Gertrude Stein and other American writers, as well as James Joyce. Returning to America, he produced his famous opera *Four Saints in Three Acts,* to a libretto by Gertrude Stein. It was given in Hartford, Connecticut, on February 8, 1934, under the auspices of the "Society of Friends and Enemies of Modern Music." Another opera to words by Gertrude Stein was *The Mother of Us All,* on the life of the American suffragette Susan B. Anthony. In 1972 he produced his opera *Byron.* He further wrote several ballets, two symphonies, four piano sonatas, two sets of etudes for piano, a cello concerto, much chamber music, and film scores. From 1940 to 1954 he was the music critic of the *New York Herald Tribune;* his brilliant personal style of writing won him many admirers.

TITL, Emil, Czech composer and conductor. He was born in Pernstein, Moravia, October 2, 1809, and died in Vienna, January 21, 1882. He was active mainly as a theater conductor, but also wrote operas, choruses, and instrumental pieces. His *Serenade* for violin became popular in various arrangements.

TOCH, Ernst, eminent Austrian composer. He was born in Vienna, December 7, 1887, and died in Los Angeles, October 1, 1964. He was entirely self-taught in musical composition. In 1909 he went to Frankfurt where he took piano lessons. In 1913 he was appointed piano instructor in Mannheim. From 1929 to 1933 he lived in Berlin. In 1935 he emigrated to the United States, settling in Los Angeles. As a composer, Toch belongs to the Modern Romantic School, distinguished by impeccable formal designs and an expressive dynamic quality. He wrote six symphonies, several chamber operas, other chamber music, a piano concerto, a cello concerto, a symphony for piano and orchestra, symphonic overtures, nine string quartets, and many works for piano solo.

TORRE, Francisco de la, Spanish sixteenth-century composer of keyboard music. His dances for various instruments enjoyed a certain vogue.

VAN SLYCK, Nicholas, American pianist and composer. He was born in Philadelphia, October 25, 1922. He studied composition at Harvard University with Walter Piston (B.A., 1946; M.A., 1948). He subsequently held numerous positions as conductor and educator and eventually was appointed director of the Longy School of Music in Cambridge, Massachusetts. He wrote a harpsichord suite, a brass quintet, three piano concertos, six piano sonatas, four song cycles, and miscellaneous works for various instruments. Among his teaching pieces for piano are *Lines and Spaces, One Cell,* and *Perspective.*

VAUGHAN WILLIAMS, Ralph, eminent English composer. He was born in Down Ampney, Gloucestershire, October 12, 1872, and died in London, August 26, 1958. He studied at Trinity College in Cambridge, obtaining his B.Mus. in 1894 and B.A. in 1895. He then went to the Royal College of Music to study composition with Parry and Stanford. Subsequently he took composition lessons with Max Bruch in Berlin. A profound believer in the validity of folk music, he undertook a thorough study of English folksongs. Many of his works are colored by folklike inflections in thematic material. Vaughan Williams wrote seven symphonies, a number of instrumental concertos including one for tuba and orchestra, oratorios and cantatas, operas, and ballets. He composed numerous choral works, hymn tunes, carols, and other vocal pieces, both sacred and secular. He was broad-minded in selecting the most fitting techniques for his compositions and showed great interest in modern developments, but steadfastly adhered to the traditional tonal principles of melodic and harmonic structures.

VERDI, Giuseppe, great Italian opera composer. He was born in Busseto, Parma, October 10, 1813, and died in Milan, January 27, 1901. He studied music with a local organist and began to compose at a very early age. In 1834 he went to Milan for regular studies. His first opera, *Oberto,* was performed at La Scala in Milan in 1839. It was followed by the operas *Nabucco* (1842), *Ernani* (1844), and others. His first undoubted masterpiece was *Rigoletto* (1851). Its success was repeated with the production of *Il Trovatore* (1853) and *La Traviata* (1853), which established Verdi's standing as a great master of opera. His reputation was reinforced by the productions of *Un Ballo in maschera* (1859), *La Forza del destino* (1862), and *Don Carlos* (1867). Verdi achieved worldwide fame with the production of *Aida,* which was premiered in Cairo on Christmas Eve of 1871 as a commission from the Khedive of Egypt to celebrate the opening of the Suez Canal. The opera marked a stylistic advance in Verdi's creative evolution, embodying elements of exotic tone painting and a greater role given to the orchestra. The event was accompanied by sensational publicity, but Verdi chose not to attend the performance. Verdi's subsequent operas, *Otello* (1887) and *Falstaff* (1893), showed a further advance in dramatic characterization. Among non-operatic works, Verdi's *Requiem Mass* is rightly admired. He also wrote some chamber music.

VILLA-LOBOS, Heitor, foremost Brazilian composer. He was born in Rio de Janeiro, March 5, 1887, and died there, November 17, 1959. He dedicated his entire creative energy to the composition of music in a national Brazilian manner. In reply to an inquiry as to the nature of folklore, he announced, "I am folklore." Indeed, his works are permeated with folklike melodic inflections and Brazilian dance rhythms. However, Villa-Lobos rarely borrowed thematic material from actual folksongs. In support of his nationalistic ideals, he wrote a series of works for various ensembles under the generic description *Chôros,* after the name of a popular dance form of Brazil. Even more pointed are his *Bachianas Brasileiras,* in which he attempted to set Brazilian motives in Bach-like counterpoint. Apart from these pieces, Villa-Lobos wrote several symphonies, much chamber music, piano pieces, and songs. He was also active as an educator and published a collection of vocal and instrumental pieces designed for teaching purposes.

WAGNER, Richard, the greatest German opera composer, creator of the "Music Drama." He was born in Leipzig, May 22, 1813, and died in Venice, February 13, 1883. He studied piano, but made little progress, and soon turned to operatic composition. He achieved his first success with *Rienzi* (1842). This was followed by *The Flying Dutchman* (1843). He reached the full maturity of his genius with *Tannhäuser* (1845). Wagner's progress was interrupted by the revolutionary events in Germany, in which he was peripherally involved; he was obliged to leave Saxony to escape arrest. He was befriended by Liszt who urged him to continue his work. Wagner then completed his great opera *Lohengrin,* which was performed by Liszt in 1850. While working on *Lohengrin,* Wagner was already preoccupied with the epic cycle of music dramas, *Der Ring des Nibelungen.* In 1865 Wagner composed his opera *Tristan und Isolde,* based on an old Cornish legend. Wagner's *Meistersinger von Nürnberg* (1868) was the only comic opera he ever wrote. His last opera was *Parsifal,* described by Wagner as "a sacred festival drama," and first performed in Bayreuth on July 26, 1882. Wagner wrote his own libretti for all of his operas which he preferred to call "Music Dramas." In order to bring out the dramatic characteristics of the action, Wagner developed a system of leitmotivs (leading motives) designating each personage and each subject as the music drama unfolds. The importance of Wagner's operatic revolution is immeasurable; not a single opera composer after Wagner escaped his influence. Wagner's traditions are maintained in the annual Bayreuth Festivals, founded in 1876, which feature complete cycles of Wagner's operas.

WALDROP, Gideon, American composer and educator. He was born in Haskell County, Texas, September 2, 1919. He studied at the Eastman School of Music in Rochester (Ph.D., 1952). From 1954 to 1958 he was the editor and general manager of *The Musical Courier*. After being affiliated with the Peabody Conservatory of Music in Baltimore and the Ford Foundation, he was appointed dean at the Juilliard School of Music in 1962. Among his works are a symphony, a trio for viola, clarinet, and harp, *Lydian Trumpeter* for trumpet and piano, *Pressures* for string orchestra, and piano pieces.

WALDTEUFEL, Emil, Alsatian composer of waltzes. He was born in Strasbourg, December 9, 1837, and died in Paris, February 16, 1915. He studied at the Paris Conservatory and, in 1865, was appointed director of the Court Balls of the Second Empire. He published 268 dances for various ensembles. Of these, *Les Patineurs* (*The Skaters*) and *Estudiantina* became perennial favorites.

WARD, Robert, American composer and conductor. He was born in Cleveland, Ohio, September 13, 1917. He studied with Howard Hanson and Bernard Rogers at the Eastman School of Music in Rochester and with Frederick Jacobi at the Juilliard School of Music. He also took courses in composition with Aaron Copland at the Berkshire Music Center. He was a member of the faculty at Columbia University and the Juilliard School of Music. Subsequently he became managing editor of the Galaxy Music Corporation and Highgate Press, a position he held until 1967 when he was appointed head of the School of Performing Arts at Winston-Salem, North Carolina. Ward has written three symphonies, nine other works for orchestra, chamber music, and piano pieces. His opera *The Crucible*, produced by the New York City Opera Company on October 26, 1961, had numerous performances in America and in Europe. His opera *The Lady from Colorado* (1964) received the Pulitzer Prize.

WARD, Samuel. A., American composer of ballads. He was born in Newark, New Jersey, in 1847 and died there in 1903. In 1882 he wrote a tune originally known as *Materna*. It was used as the setting of the poem *O Mother Dear* in 1888, and became famous when Katherine Lee Bates (1859–1929), professor of English Literature at Wellesley College, used it, in turn, as a setting of her poem *America the Beautiful*. The writing of the poem was inspired by her contemplation of the spacious landscape viewed from the summit of Pike's Peak in Colorado.

WARREN, George William, American organist and hymn writer. He was born in Albany, New York, August 17, 1828, and died in New York City, March 17, 1902. He served as church organist, his last position being at St. Thomas' in New York. In 1888 he published "Warren's Hymns and Tunes as sung at St. Thomas' Church." His tune entitled *National Hymn* is the setting of the popular hymn *God of Our Fathers*.

WASHBURN, Robert, American composer. He was born in Bouckville, New York, July 11, 1928. He attended the State University College of Potsdam, New York. After service in the U.S. Air Force, he returned to Potsdam and joined its faculty. He received his Ph.D. at the Eastman School of Music in Rochester. Washburn wrote orchestral works, chamber music, choruses, and instrumental solos. Among his teaching pieces for piano are *Black Keys, Follow the Leader, Up and Down*, and *Valse Triste*.

WATSON, Scott, American pianist and composer. He was born in Etowah, Tennessee, November 22, 1915. He studied music at the Peabody Institute in Baltimore and subsequently taught there. In 1972 he was Head of Music at Oldfields School in Glencoe, Maryland. He wrote some effective teaching pieces for piano, among them *Fiddlestrings, London Bells*, and *Parade Time*.

WAXMAN, Donald, American composer and teacher. He was born in Steubenville, Ohio, October 29, 1925. He studied at the Juilliard School of Music, then founded a private music school in Nyack, New York. He wrote a number of easy piano pieces with romantic titles, among them *Three Conversations: Friendly, Angry, Jolly, On a Summer Afternoon, Sad Daydream*, and *The Tiny Mouse*. Some of his pieces are exotic in character, such as *The Rajah's Dance*.

WEBB, George James, American organist and editor. He was born in Rushmore Lodge, near Salisbury, England, June 24, 1803, and died in Orange, New Jersey, October 7, 1887. He settled in America in 1830 and played organ at the Old South Church in Boston. In 1870 he went to live in New Jersey. He also gave music courses in New York. He edited a number of musical publications and anthologies, and is best known for his hymn tune *Stand Up, Stand Up for Jesus*.

WEBER, Carl Maria von, celebrated German composer, one of the forerunners of German Romanticism in music. He was born in Eutin, November 18, 1786, and died in London, June 5, 1826. He went to Salzburg as a youth and had theory lessons with Michael Haydn. He made extraordinary progress, toured as a concert pianist in German provinces, and occupied various posts as opera director. His operatic masterpiece was *Der Freischütz*, of which he conducted the first performance at the Berlin Opera on June 18, 1821. The opera, with its fantastic libretto, is regarded by music historians as inaugurating the Romantic age in music. Weber's second opera, *Euryanthe*, was produced in Vienna in 1823. After its success, Weber was commissioned by Covent Garden in London to write an opera in English, *Oberon*. Webern conducted it in London on April 12, 1826. His health, undermined by tuberculosis, broke, and he died in London at the age of thirty-nine.

WEBERN, Anton, great composer of the modern Viennese School. He was born in Vienna, December 3, 1883, and died in Mittersill, September 15, 1945, in a tragic accident: he was shot by an American military guard when he failed to halt after curfew. Webern was a student and disciple of Arnold Schoenberg with whom he organized a society for private musical performances in Vienna in order to promote new music. Webern's early works, some of them recently discovered, are in a romantic vein. In his desire to attain a maximum of expressive power, Webern experimented with miniature forms in an atonal idiom. He adopted the twelve-tone method of composition after it was promulgated by Schoenberg. Webern wrote only a few works but they acquired great significance in the subsequent evolution of modern music.

WERDER, Richard, American pianist, composer, and teacher. He was born in Williamsburg, Iowa, December 21, 1919. He studied at the Juilliard School of Music and at Teachers College, Columbia University, from which he received his M.A. and Ed. D. degrees. Subsequently he joined the music department at the Catholic University of America in Washington, D.C. He composed a number of pedagogical pieces for piano, among them *Black on White, The Drum, Procession of the Pachyderms, Resting Time,* and *Down, Up.*

WILLIAMS, Alberto, Argentinian composer. He was born in Buenos Aires, November 23, 1862, and died there, June 17, 1952. His grandfather was an Englishman who settled in Argentina. Alberto Williams studied composition in Paris with Guiraud, Durand, and Godard, and organ with César Franck. Returning to Argentina in 1889, he founded a number of music schools and a publishing house. He wrote nine symphonies and a great many piano pieces in the rhythms of national Argentinian dances.

WILLIS, Richard S., American composer of religious hymns and patriotic songs. He was born in Boston, February 10, 1819, and died in Detroit, May 7, 1900. He went to Germany to study music. Upon his return to America, he edited anthologies of church hymns. Of his own songs, the most popular is the Christmas carol *It Came Upon the Midnight Clear,* which he wrote in 1850.

WINNER, Septimus, American composer of songs and ballads. He was born in Philadelphia, May 11, 1827, and died there, November 22, 1902. He owned a music store in Philadelphia, and gave music lessons on the violin and the banjo. In 1854 he published his best known song, *Listen to the Mockingbird.* Another popular song by Winner is *Dutch Warbler.*

WINOGRON, Blanche, American harpsichordist, composer, and editor. She was born in New York, May 8, 1911, and studied at Hunter College, receiving her B.A. in music and languages. She also took piano lessons with Anne Hull and studied composition with Henry Holden Huss, Walter Helfer, Stefan Wolpe, and Felix Salzer. She subsequently conducted adult teaching programs at the Greenwich House Settlement School in New York, was on the faculty of the Mannes College of Music from 1958 to 1968, and then joined the faculty at the New England Conservatory of Music in Boston. She published several teaching pieces for piano and edited two volumes of historical keyboard literature for the New Scribner Music Library. (*For additional biographical information see Volume 2.*)

WOLF, Hugo, great Austrian composer, master of the Late-Romantic Lied. He was born in Windisch-Gräz, March 13, 1860, and died in Vienna, February 22, 1903. He studied at the Vienna Conservatory and became an ardent advocate of the music of Wagner and Liszt. He wrote Lieder to texts by Goethe, Heine, and other German poets. He was also active as a music critic. The distinguishing characteristic of Hugo Wolf's songs is an opulent piano accompaniment, often written in an intricate, contrapuntal style. As a result, he has been described by some as the "Wagner of the Lied." His personal life was tragic: mentally unstable and socially intractable, he attempted suicide, and eventually had to be taken to an insane asylum where he died at the age of forty-two.

WOODBURY, Isaac Baker, American song composer. He was born in Beverly, Massachusetts, October 23, 1819, and died in Charleston, South Carolina, October 26, 1858. He was a blacksmith by trade, but was fond of music and went to Europe for his musical education. Returning to America, he was active as a teacher and editor of music magazines. He published several anthologies of sacred songs. Of his own pieces, *Stars of the Summer Night* is notable.

YAMADA, Kôsçak, outstanding Japanese composer. He was born in Tokyo, June 9, 1886, and died there, December 29, 1965. He studied in Berlin with Max Bruch. Returning to Japan in 1914, he was active as conductor, educator, and composer. He wrote several operas based on Japanese subjects. His dance movements are notable for the authenticity of their thematic materials.

YRADIER, Sebastián, Spanish song composer. He was born in Sauciego, Alava, January 20, 1809, and died in Vitoria, December 6, 1865. He was active mainly as a composer of theater music and songs. For a time, he lived in Paris and in Cuba. In 1859 he published *La Paloma,* a song described as a "canción Americana," which became a perennial favorite, often mistaken for a folksong. Bizet borrowed Yradier's song *El Areglito* for the tune of the famous *Habanera* from *Carmen.*

ZUCCALMAGLIO, Florentin von, German folksong collector and composer. He was born in Waldbröl, April 12, 1803, and died in Nachrodt, Westphalia, March 23, 1869. He was not a professional musician, but wrote articles in music journals and published collections of German folksongs. Some melodies in these anthologies were by Zuccalmaglio himself.

Reference Dictionary of Musical Terms

COMPILED BY NICOLAS SLONIMSKY

A. The note a major sixth above middle C; it traditionally serves for tuning an orchestra.

Absolute Pitch. An innate ability to name any note, or the notes of any chord, with unfailing accuracy. Not every person possessing absolute pitch is necessarily superior to other musicians; it is a gift that cannot be taught or developed. Also called Perfect Pitch.

A cappella. Literally, "as in a chapel;" unaccompanied choral singing.

A capriccio. Capricious; fanciful.

Accelerando. Accelerating; increasing in speed.

Accidental. A sharp or flat not belonging to the key signature; also a natural.

Accompaniment. A series of chords or other harmonic units, supporting the melody.

Accordion. A popular instrument held in both hands, with two manuals, one with piano-like keys for the right hand, and one with buttons for playing the harmony in the left hand. The sound is produced by compressing and pulling out the bellows between the two manuals, thus forcing air through slots with flexible metal tongues called reeds, and causing the reeds to vibrate.

Adagio. Very slow.

Ad libitum. (Ad lib.) Freely interpreted; improvised.

Affettuoso. With affection; tenderly.

Affrettando. Becoming faster; with nervous animation.

Agitato. Agitated; speeded up.

Air. A song; a songful instrumental piece.

Aleatory Music. Also called Chance Music. An important modern type of music in which not only the composer, but also the performers are involved in the process of composing, since they must exercise their own creative imagination according to composer-directed rules and instructions. While the composer usually provides the basic musical and structural ingredients, the details of their interpretation are arrived at by various chance means ranging from intuition to random schemes, such as throwing dice, electronic manipulations, and "game plans." The notation is often deliberately vague, to assure different interpretations at each performance. In jazz, the jam session is, to some extent, an aleatory "event." The word aleatory is derived from the Latin *alea*, "a game of dice."

Al fine. Literally, "to the finish;" used in phrases like *Dal segno al fine* (from the sign to the end marked *Fine*).

Alla. "In the manner of," as in *alla zingarese* (in a gypsy manner).

Allargando. Gradually becoming slower.

Allegretto. Literally, "a little *Allegro;*" a tempo not quite as fast as *Allegro*.

Allegro. Lively; a rather fast tempo.

Allegro ma non troppo. "Fast, but not too fast."

Alleluia. Literally, "Praise the Lord!" Also *Hallelujah*.

Allemande. The first movement of the instrumental suite of the Baroque era, in 4/4 time. The word *Allemande* means "German" in French, but the character of the movement is not necessarily Germanic.

Alto. Literally, "high." In choral singing, the word *alto* applies to female (or boys') voices in a range below soprano. Alto clef, with middle C on the third line, is used for the viola part.

Amoroso. Amorous; with an affectionate touch.

Ancora. Yet, or still. *Ancora più mosso* means "still more quickly."

Andante. Literally, "going," or "walking." *Andante* is the tempo suggesting an easy walking pace.

Andantino. Literally, "a little Andante;" a tempo a little less deliberate than *Andante*.

Animato. Animated.

A piacere. "As you please," that is, free in tempo and dynamics.

Appassionato. Impassioned. *Appassionata* (with a feminine ending) is the title of Beethoven's piano sonata, opus 57, descriptive of its impassioned character.

Appoggiatura. Literally, "a leaning." An accented non-harmonic tone forming a dissonance with the principal chord.

Arabesque. A melodic ornament suggesting an Arabian tune. Also a Romantic composition abounding in such patterns.

Arco. Literally, "bow." A term applied in the notation for string instruments, instructing the performer to "play with the bow" (after having played *pizzicato*).

Aria. Literally, "an air." A song; applied particularly to a solo in an opera.

Arioso. "Like an aria;" a song less formal than an aria.

Armonioso. Harmonious.

Arpeggiato. Performed as if played on the harp (*arpa*), i.e., as a broken chord.

Arpeggio. A broken chord, as played on the harp. From the Italian word *arpa*, "the harp."

Arrangement. A transcription of a work for a solo instrument or for a combination of instruments different from those for which the piece was originally written.

As. German for A-flat.

Assai. Very; as in *Allegro assai* (very fast).

A tempo. A directive to resume the original speed, usually after a slower or ad lib. section, or after a *ritardando*.

Atonality. The absence of tonality. This term is used to describe the type of modern composition in which the traditional structures of tonal melody, harmony, and modulation are abandoned, and the key signature is absent.

Attacca. An imperative, "attack;" that is, "go on without a pause."

Aubade. The French word for "morning music;" from *aube,* "the dawn."

Autoharp. A zither-like educational instrument having devices for playing pre-set chords; used to demonstrate harmonic progressions and to accompany simple songs.

Auxiliary note. A side-note one degree above or below the harmony note.

B. German for B-flat. *B dur* is B-flat major; *B moll* is B-flat minor.

Badinerie. French word for "teasing;" occasionally used in Baroque music as the title of a quick movement in 2/4 time.

Bagatelle. Literally, "a trifle;" a short composition, usually for piano solo.

Bagpipe. Scottish portable wind instrument in which the air is blown by bellows.

Balalaika. A popular Russian instrument not unlike a mandolin or guitar, but triangular in shape, usually with three strings.

Ballad. A song of a narrative nature, with a dramatic or sentimental text.

Ballade. An instrumental composition of a romantic nature, usually for piano.

Ballet. A theatrical group dance usually illustrating a dramatic action by means of expressive movements and gestures, accompanied by specially composed music, or adapted to a previously existing musical work.

Band. An orchestral group, composed of wind instruments and drums, as in Brass Band, Military Band, and Dance Band.

Banjo. American folk instrument with five strings plucked by fingers, made popular in Negro spirituals, hillbilly music, and early jazz.

Bar. The dividing line (barline) between two measures; also a measure of music itself.

Barbershop Harmony. A type of close harmony arrangement, stylized from amateur performances by singing barbers in America at the turn of the century.

Barcarole. A boating song; from the Italian words *barca* (bark) and *rollo* (rower). Also spelled Barcarolle.

Baritone. The male voice higher in pitch than the bass voice, but lower than the tenor. Also a small tuba used in band music.

Baroque. The style of classical composition, vocal and instrumental, embracing the period from about 1600 to 1750. Although the word Baroque originally meant bizarre, it has acquired with the passage of time the almost opposite sense of dignified and precise craftsmanship.

Baroque Organ. A church organ in common use during the Baroque period, associated particularly with the organ works of Bach. Although much lighter in sound than the modern organ, it possesses a penetrating tonal quality which renders it entirely capable of creating the necessary melodic and harmonic effects.

Baroque Suite. An instrumental suite of dance forms, also called the Classical Suite. It has four principal movements: Allemande, Courante, Sarabande, and Gigue. Lighter dance movements, such as the Minuet, Bourrée, and Gavotte, are often interpolated between the Sarabande and the Gigue.

Barrel Organ. A pipe organ with a number of mechanically prearranged tunes, played by itinerant street peddlers by means of rotating a handle to activate the mechanism. Also erroneously called Hurdy-Gurdy, a cranked string instrument.

Bass. The lowest male voice; the lowest part in harmony; the lowest tone of a chord.

Bass Clef. The clef indicating the position of F below middle C on the fourth line of the staff.

Basset Horn. A clarinet in F which sounds a fifth lower than the written note.

Bass Fiddle. A colloquial name for the Double Bass.

Basso. Italian for "bass;" used mostly to describe a deep male voice; *Basso profondo,* a bass voice of a particularly low range.

Basso Continuo. *see* Continuo.

Bassoon. A woodwind instrument, the lowest of the woodwind group, with a range from B-flat below the staff of the bass clef to about three octaves upwards. The range of the Double Bassoon is one octave lower.

Basso ostinato. Literally, "obstinate bass." The term is applied to a constantly recurring bass; also called ground bass or simply ground (old English grownde).

Beat. A unit of musical time in a measure.

Beguine. A Latin American dance in a lively syncopated rhythm.

Bel canto. Literally, "beautiful singing;" a lyric and precisely articulated singing style particularly identified with Italian opera.

Bémol. French for "flat."

Ben. Short for *bene* (well); used in phrases like *ben marcato* (well marked), *ben tenuto* (well sustained), etc.

Berceuse. French word for a lullaby.

Bewegt. German for moving, animated.

Binary Form. A musical construction consisting of two distinctly recognizable sections and ending necessarily in the tonic. The Gavotte and the Allemande are examples of Binary Form.

Bis. Twice; commonly used in Europe to request an encore.

Blue Note. The lowered seventh in the Blues and early jazz.

Blues. A somewhat wistful American Negro ballad, in 4/4 time, often with the characteristic lowered seventh, or "blue" note.

Bolero. A rhythmic Spanish dance in vivacious triple time enlivened by cross accents.

Bourrée. A quick French dance in duple time, which forms a part of the instrumental suite of the Baroque era.

Brass Band. An ensemble consisting only of brass instruments, occasionally including drums.

Bravo. A shout of acclaim for the performer, commonly used to hail an opera singer. The feminine form is *brava*.

Bravura. Literally, "swashbuckling," bold swagger. In music, *bravura* signifies a resounding display of technical virtuosity.

Breve. Italian word which literally means "short." *Alla breve* means "double-quick time" in 4/4 and is notated by a vertical line drawn through the capital letter C: ¢. (Actually 2/2 time.)

Brindisi. A drinking song.

Brio. Vigorous brilliance; used mostly in the phrase *con brio* (with vigor, or with brilliance).

Broken Chord. A harmony unit played in *arpeggio* form, either as a self-contained progression or as an accompaniment.

Bugle. A natural brass instrument, usually tuned in B-flat, and producing only the notes of the harmonic series.

Burlesca. A display piece of instrumental music marked by ornamental brilliance.

Burlesque. A light piece of singing entertainment; a brilliant but inconsequential instrumental composition.

Cabaletta. In Italian opera, the concluding section of an aria, forming a sort of summary in rapid tempo.

Cachucha. A Spanish dance in quick triple time; a rustic form of the Bolero.

Cadence. An ending. The most common cadence consists of the dominant and tonic chords, called an authentic cadence. When the chord preceding the tonic is the subdominant, the cadence is called plagal.

Cadenza. An elaborate solo display of an improvisatory character in an instrumental concerto, or sonata, often played *ad libitum*.

Cakewalk. An American Negro folk dance in ragtime rhythms.

Calando. Gradually becoming softer and slower.

Calliope. A circus organ with very loud whistles activated by steam.

Calmato. Calming down.

Calmo. Calm, tranquil.

Canarie. A dance in triple time, supposedly imitating the rhythms of the native music of the Canary Islands.

Cancan. A fast French vaudeville dance in 2/4 time, once regarded as extremely naughty.

Canon. A contrapuntal composition in which voices enter in strict imitation, one after another, either in the same pitch, or an octave apart (canon in unison), or at some other interval apart. For ex., in a canon at the fifth, the imitating voice enters one fifth higher or lower than the original voice.

Canonic. In the manner of a canon; containing imitation of the main theme in another voice.

Cantabile. In a songful manner.

Cantando. Singingly.

Cantata. Literally, a "piece that is sung." A choral work, usually with soloists, with an orchestral accompaniment.

Cantilena. A type of singing in a smoothly flowing manner.

Canto. A song.

Cantus firmus. Literally, "a firm chant." A theme or a subject which is treated as the principal part of a contrapuntal composition. A cantus firmus is usually placed in the tenor, but may also occur in any other voice.

Canzona. The word actually means "a song," but in Baroque and early Classical usage it was also applied to an instrumental piece of a songful nature, as well as to an early form of the fugue.

Canzonetta. Literally, "a little *canzona*." A song for a single voice, or several voices; by extension, a brief instrumental piece.

Capriccio. A fanciful composition in the Baroque style, marked by vivacious rhythms. Also Caprice, in English.

Capriccioso. Capricious, whimsical.

Carillon. A set of chimes played by way of a keyboard attachment. A composition imitating bells.

Carol. A Christmas song.

Castanets. Spanish clackers held in a dancer's hand and clicked in rhythm to the dance.

Cavatina. A short operatic aria.

Celesta. A keyboard instrument with hammers striking metal bars mounted on a soundboard, producing bell-like sounds. Its compass is only four octaves, from middle C upwards.

Cello. *see* Violoncello.

Cembalo. Abbreviation for Clavicembalo (Harpsichord).

Chaconne. A contrapuntal form of composition consisting of a series of variations on a theme in a definite harmonic progression. The Chaconne is close in structure to the Passacaglia.

Chamber Music. A category of works written for small groups of players, numbering from two to nine (duos, trios, quartets, quintets, sextets, septets, octets, nonets).

Chamber Symphony. A work scored for a small orchestra and usually shorter than the standard symphony.

Chance Music. *see* Aleatory Music.

Chanson. French word for "song." In the Renaissance period, the word also applied to polyphonic compositions.

Character Piece. A common description for a brief composition, usually for piano, portraying a scene, or expressing a mood, for instance Bagatelle, Impromptu, Moment Musical, Novelette. Also called "Characteristic Piece."

Choir. A church chorus. The term choir is also applied to instrumental groups in the orchestra, as in "brass choir."

Chorale. A hymn tune sung by a church congregation or by a choir.

Chorale Prelude. An instrumental composition based on a chorale (hymn) tune.

Chord. A combination of several notes played simultaneously; a harmony.

Chôros. A Brazilian folk dance, or a work written in a Brazilian folk style.

Chorus. An ensemble of voices, consisting of sopranos, altos, tenors, and basses (abbreviated SATB); a female or boys' chorus consists of sopranos and altos; a male chorus consists of tenors, baritones, and basses. The word chorus is also used for a refrain in popular songs, show tunes, and similar light music.

Chromatic. A progression of notes in semitones, or half-steps.

Cis. German for C-sharp.

Clarinet. A transposing woodwind instrument possessing a clear, far-carrying sound, with a range of more than three octaves. The B-flat clarinet is the most common; it transposes a whole-step down, so that a notated C sounds B-flat. The lowest note of the clarinet is notated E, which sounds D on the B-flat clarinet and C-sharp on the clarinet in A. The Bass Clarinet is one octave lower than the standard clarinet. There is also a high clarinet in E-flat in which the notated C sounds E-flat above the written note.

Classical Music. Broadly, the music of the 17th and 18th centuries, marked by symmetry of form and nobility of content. The term is also used colloquially to describe serious music of any kind, as opposed to popular music.

Classical Suite. *see* Baroque Suite.

Clavecin. French for Harpsichord.

Claves. Hardwood sticks used in Latin American rhythm bands, which produce a sharp sound when clicked together.

Clavicembalo. Harpsichord; Cembalo.

Clavichord. An early keyboard instrument in which the strings are impinged by metal tangents, producing a soft, briefly sustained sound.

Clavier. French for Klavier (piano, or keyboard instrument in general).

Clef. Literally, "key;" a sign on the staff indicating the position of a certain note on the staff.

Close Harmony. A type of harmonization in which the upper voices are arranged in as close a formation as possible.

Coda. The conclusion of a composition. The coda is sometimes quite extensive and often contains materials derived from principal themes. The word itself means "tail" in Italian.

Codetta. Literally, "a little tail." A short coda.

Col. The same as *con* (with); used in such phrases as *col legno* (with the back of the bow).

Col canto. "With the song." An instruction to the accompanist to follow the singer sympathetically in every nuance or in every variation of tempo.

Colla voce. "With the voice;" the same as *col canto*.

Coloratura. A colorful and florid display of singing virtuosity. A coloratura soprano is a singer possessing great skill in vocalization in high register.

Come Prima. "As before." An indication that the tempo and expression should be similar to a previous section of the same character.

Comic Opera. An operetta. Originally, opera with spoken dialogue; even a highly dramatic, serious opera with spoken passages (particularly in France) was called *opéra comique* (comic opera).

Common Chord. A colloquial term for a major triad.

Common Time. A colloquial term for 4/4 time, often notated with the capital letter C, which derives from a semicircle, the medieval symbol for duple time.

Comodo. Accommodating, leisurely.

Compound Meter. A measure consisting of two unequal units, as 5/8 (3/8 + 2/8).

Con. "With;" used in many phrases, such as *con moto* (with motion), *con brio* (with brilliance).

Con amore. Literally, "with love;" affectionately, tenderly.

Con brio. With brilliance.

Concert. A public or semi-public performance by a soloist, an ensemble, a choral group, a band, or a symphony orchestra. A solo concert is often called a recital.

Concertante. A composition or section played in the manner of a solo performance with an orchestral accompaniment; less specific than a concerto; having a less prominent solo part than a concerto.

Concertina. A popular instrument, similar to the Accordion, but having only buttons (instead of keys *and* buttons).

Concertino. A little concerto, scored for a small ensemble. In Baroque music, a small group of instruments representing a collective solo within the total orchestra (*see* Concerto Grosso).

Concertmaster. The soloist of the first violin section in an orchestra, who sits on the right side at the first desk of his section.

Concerto. A composition for a solo instrument accompanied by an orchestra.

Concerto for Orchestra. A symphonic work in which the entire orchestra and its individual instruments or instrument choirs play the role of soloists.

Concerto Grosso. Literally, "a grand concerto." A Baroque form in which a select group of instruments, called Concertino, plays the role of a collective soloist.

Concert Pitch. The actual sound (not the written note) of a transposing instrument.

Conductor. The chief coordinator of the performance of an orchestra, or an opera, who stands in front, with his back to the audience, indicating with his baton (in modern times often with his bare hands) and with his facial expressions the time, the rhythm, and the dynamic gradations. The conductor's left hand is sometimes called "expression hand" because it governs the instrumental balance and the finer nuances in the performance.

Con espressione. With expression.

Con moto. With motion; moving along.

Console. The keyboard section of an organ. It includes the manuals, pedals, stops, auxiliary devices such as couplers, swells, etc., and the music rack.

Consonance. The combination of two or three different tones, producing only consonant intervals, i.e., thirds, fourths, fifths, and sixths.

Continuo. The bass part in a pre-Classical (mostly Baroque) composition, to which a keyboard performer adds proper harmonies, etc. At times, these harmonies are notated by means of a system of figures indicating the intervals from the bass tones up. Such continuo parts are called Figured Bass parts. In modern editions, the harmonies are usually filled in by the editor, and the completed continuo parts are called "realizations."

Contrabass. Double-Bass.

Contrabassoon. Double-Bassoon.

Contralto. A female voice in the low range, identical with Alto.

Contrapuntal. Written with an emphatic application of counterpoint.

Cool Jazz. An intense type of jazz, externally restrained but inwardly possessing an enormous emotional potential.

Corda. A string. *Una corda* (one string) is a notation in piano music, instructing the player to use the soft pedal, so that the hammers strike only one string instead of three in the middle register. *Tre corde* (three strings) is a directive to release the soft pedal.

Cornet. A predecessor of the modern trumpet, having a wider bore; often used in military and concert bands.

Corrente. The Italian word for *courante*.

Counterpoint. A technique of composition of long and honorable ancestry, in which individual voices form a polyphonic web of considerable intricacy, as distinct from harmonic (chordal) writing.

Countertenor. A very high male voice; also called male alto.

Courante. A fairly rapid French dance in triple time, forming a part of the Baroque suite.

Crescendo. Gradually growing louder and louder.

Crotchet. British term for a quarter-note.

Da Capo. Literally, "from the beginning;" a directive to go back to the beginning and repeat until the mark *Fine* (finish). *Da capo al fine* (*D.C. al fine*) means "from the beginning to the finish." Sometimes abbreviated *D.C.*

Dal Segno. "From the sign;" usually in the phrase *Dal segno al fine* (from the sign until the measure marked *Fine*). Sometimes abbreviated *D.S.*

D.C. Abbreviation for *Da capo*.

Decrescendo. The opposite to *crescendo*, i.e., gradually diminishing in loudness.

Degree. A whole-step or a half-step in the diatonic scale.

Demisemiquaver. British term for one half of a sixteenth-note, i.e., a thirty-second note.

Des. German for D-flat.

Détaché. Detached; applied to bowing on a string instrument in separate strokes.

Development. The middle section in a sonata movement, in which the principal themes appear in various keys.

Diatonic. A sequence of tones following the degrees of the scale in ordered whole-steps and half-steps; not chromatic.

Dièze. French for sharp.

Diminuendo. Gradually diminishing in loudness.

Dis. German for D-sharp.

Dissonance. A discordant combination of sounds, containing dissonant intervals, such as seconds and sevenths, and requiring a resolution into a consonance.

Divertimento. Literally, "a diversion, entertainment." A term applied to a composition containing several unconnected movements designed to entertain.

Divisi (Div.). Divided; an indication that a specific instrumental section, particularly in the strings, is to be split into two or more sections playing different parts.

Do. In Latin countries, and in Russia, the note C.

Dodecaphonic. A learned description of twelve-tone music. The term is derived from the Greek word *dodeca* (twelve).

Dolce. Sweet.

Dolcissimo. Very sweet.

Dolente. Wistful; sad.

Doloroso. Dolorous; sorrowful.

Dominant. The fifth note of a scale.

Doppio. Double; as in *doppio movimento* (double speed).

D.S. Abbreviation for *Dal segno*.

Double-Bass. The lowest string instrument, and the largest in size. Its four strings are tuned in fourths: E, A, D, G. Double-Bass is sometimes called String Bass or Bass Viol. Some Double-Basses have an additional low C string.

Double-Bassoon. Wind instrument with a range one octave lower than the Bassoon.

Double Concerto. Concerto for two instruments and orchestra.

Doucement. Gently.

Duet. A composition for two performers.

Duple Time. Time signature with the numerator 2 or 4, as in 2/4, 4/8, or 4/4; also applied to measures with two main beats, as 6/4 and 6/8.

Dur. German term for major, as in *C dur* (C major), *F dur* (F major), etc.

Electronic Music. Originally music consisting of collages of live, recorded sounds which had been electronically altered, superimposed, and otherwise manipulated. Today mostly the type of modern music generated by specially constructed electronic instruments capable of producing any desired pitch, any scale, any rhythm, any tone color, and any degree of loudness, etc., thereby greatly expanding the resources of music making. The most advanced electronic instruments are the Synthesizers.

Elegy. A lament; a memorial composition for the dead.

Embellishments. Ornaments, such as trills, appoggiaturas, etc.

Encore. An extra piece played at the end of a concert in response to applause. The word means "again" in French.

En dehors. Literally, "outside." The term means "to bring out" (the melody).

Energico. Energetic.

English Horn. Alto oboe in F, sounding a fifth lower than the written note. It has a penetrating, somewhat nasal sound.

Enharmonic. The same note differently written, such as D-flat versus C-sharp.

Ensemble. A group of instrumentalists.

Es. German for E-flat.

Espressione. Expression; used in the phrase *con espressione* (with expression).

Espressivo. Expressively; often abbreviated "*espr.*" The term signifies that the melody should be brought out with great emotional expression.

Etude. A finger exercise. In more extensive usage, a virtuoso piece of instrumental music, allowing a brilliant technical display.

Exposition. The opening of a sonata movement, in which the principal themes are presented for the first time.

Expressionism. A modern musical style of the first half of the twentieth century, which deliberately opposed the style of Impressionism that preceded it: instead of creating highly sensitive, sweetly blurred, atmospheric mood pictures, Expressionism soberly focused on strictly musical phenomena, introducing the harsh dissonances of atonality, irregular rhythms, and clashing instrumental sonorities, calculated to recapture the intrinsic power of music.

Expression marks. Annotations in the musical score, indicating the manner of performance, by tradition predominantly in Italian, as *espressivo, sempre ritardando, crescendo,* etc.

f. Abbreviation for *forte* (loud).

Fa. In Latin countries, and in Russia, the note F.

Falsetto. A method of male singing in a "false" high register, often intended for comic effects.

Fandango. A vivacious Spanish dance in triple time.

Fanfare. A short flourish of ceremonial trumpets or cornets announcing a momentous occasion.

Fantaisie. French for fantasy. In Italian the spelling is "fantasia;" in German "Fantasie." A piece of music full of fancy. The Baroque and the Classical Fantaisie, however, is quite formal in its design, cast in rigorous counterpoint, with an elaborate development.

F-Clef. Bass-clef, indicating the position of F below middle C, on the fourth line of the staff.

Fermata. Literally, "a stop." A free, brief pause or an extension of the duration of a note or rest.

Festival. A series of concerts united by some general purpose or devoted to a single composer.

ff. Abbreviation for *fortissimo* (very loud).

fff. Abbreviation for *fortississimo* (very, very loud).

Fiddle. A colloquial term for the violin.

Fife. A flute used in military bands; it is tuned differently from the orchestral flute.

Figured Bass. *see* Continuo.

Finale. The final movement, usually in a festive vein, of a symphony, an instrumental suite, or an act in an opera. The concluding section of Beethoven's Ninth Symphony is a choral finale.

Fine. "Finish." This word is often placed at the end of a middle section when there is a partial repeat, indicated by the words *Da capo al fine.*

Fioritura. A flowery vocal ornament. *Fiore* is Italian for flower.

Fis. German for F-sharp.

Flat. A sign indicating the lowering of a pitch by a semitone (half-step).

Flourish. A brief fanfare, usually played by trumpets.

Flute. One of the most ancient musical instruments; sometimes called transverse flute to distinguish it from the vertical flute or recorder. Its compass ranges from middle C up three octaves. The Alto Flute transposes a fourth below the ordinary flute. The Piccolo (complete name *Flauto piccolo,* little flute) sounds one octave higher than the ordinary flute.

Folk Music. A comprehensive term covering folk dances and folksongs. Folk music is generated spontaneously among the people; its melodies and rhythms express the most profound essence of national cultures. Some songs by popular composers, such as *Dixie, Dark Eyes, Estrellita,* etc., are erroneously described as folksongs.

Form. In music, a concept of organization governing the order, character, meter, and key of a composition. The most elementary form is binary, in which only two elements are presented. Ternary form evolves from binary by the interpolation of a middle section. In a large work, such as a sonata or a symphony, formal elements often intermingle and are distinguished by their similarities or contrasts.

Forte. Strong; loud. Abbreviated *f.*

Fortissimo. Very loud. Abbreviated *ff.*

Fortississimo. Very, very loud. Abbreviated *fff.*

French Horn. A brass instrument in the shape of a coil; it is the most songful instrument of the brass section, corresponding to the tenor voice in its cantilena. Historically, it is the offspring of the hunting horn. It is usually in F and sounds a fifth below the written notes in the treble clef, or a fourth above those in the bass clef. Its range is three and one half octaves.

Fugato. A brief passage in fugal style.

Fugue. The most richly developed and intricate form of contrapuntal music. A fugue opens with a statement of the subject, which is imitated by a second voice, usually in the transposition to the dominant. The third entry returns to the tonic, and so on in alternation depending on the number of voices. After the entries are completed, the themes appear in several different tonalities, often in truncated forms, leading to a coda in which the main subject is restated in its original key. A *stretto* (an overlapping of voices in close canonic succession) is often used in the coda.

Funebre. Funereal; mournful. *Marcia funebre* is a funeral march.

Fuoco. "Fire;" used in the phrase, *con fuoco* (with fire, fiery).

Furioso. With fury; greatly excited.

Gamba. *see* Viola da gamba.

Gavotte. A classical dance in 4/4 time, usually beginning with a two-quarter upbeat; often inserted in the Baroque suite.

G-Clef. The treble-clef in which the position of G above middle C is indicated on the second line. The shape of the G-clef is a Gothic elaboration of the capital letter G.

General Pause. A bar or two of rest for the entire orchestra.

Gigue. A rapid dance, usually in 6/8 time, serving as a concluding movement of the Baroque suite.

Giocoso. Fancifully humorous.

Gis. German for G-sharp.

Giusto. Literally, "just, correct." The term is used mostly in *Tempo giusto* (just, strict tempo).

Glissando. This term is a hybrid of the French word, *glisser* (to slide) and the Italian ending *ando,* and means "slidingly." A *glissando* can easily be performed on any string instrument, on the trombone, and with effort on the clarinet. On the piano, *glissando* requires care not to bruise the thumb with which the *glissando* is usually effected.

Glockenspiel. A percussion instrument consisting of metal-bars struck with mallets.

Gong. A percussion instrument consisting of a large, suspended metal disk with a center dome. It is similar to, but not identical with, the Tamtam.

Grace Note. An extra note written in smaller size before the principal note, to be performed as an appoggiatura, or as a very short embellishment, without affecting the tempo.

Grandioso. In a grand manner; solemnly.

Grand Opera. A type of opera, usually in five acts, treating a heroic, mythological, or historical subject, sumptuously costumed, and produced in a large opera house.

Grand Piano. A large piano with a keyboard-range of seven octaves and a third (88 keys).

Graphic Notation. *see* Notation.

Grave. In a slow, ponderous tempo; gravely.

Gravicembalo. More correctly, *Clavicembalo;* a Cembalo; a Harpsichord.

Grazioso. Gracefully.

Gregorian Chant. The practice of singing religious chants according to a set of rules codified by Pope Gregory in the sixth century; often applied imprecisely to all forms of plainchant.

Ground Bass. An ostinato figure in the bass, that serves as the main subject in the Chaconne and Passacaglia.

Guitar. A universally popular string instrument, plucked by fingers, and usually having six strings. The electric guitar, amplifying the sound at will, is commonly used by dance bands and rock 'n' roll groups.

H. The German designation of B-natural. *H-dur* is B major; *H moll* is B minor.

Habanera. A Cuban dance marked by a syncopated beat in 2/4 time. The name comes from Habana (Havana); the spelling Habañera (with a tilde over *n*) is common but wrong.

Harmonica. A Mouth Organ.

Harmonics. *see* Overtones.

Harmonium. *see* Reed Organ.

Harmony. An arrangement of different tones in vertical formation, either consonant or dissonant; chords and chord progressions.

Harp. A string instrument which stands up erect, with a sound resembling that of the piano and covering a similar range. It is peculiarly adapted for playing arpeggios (a word itself derived from the Italian *arpa,* the harp).

Harpsichord. An old keyboard instrument, predecessor of the modern piano, with strings plucked by a plectrum when a key is struck, and often having two keyboards. Its range was only four and a half octaves. Its Italian name is *Clavicembalo,* commonly abbreviated to *Cembalo,* a designation which is also often used in old instrumental scores to indicate *basso continuo. Clavecin* is the French word for the harpsichord. (It is different from the *Clavichord,* in which the strings are not plucked but are impinged upon.) There has been a vigorous revival of the harpsichord in modern times, with many instruments specially manufactured according to old models.

Helicon. A large Bass Tuba which is coiled around the body of the performer. The name comes from the word *helical* (spiral-shaped).

Hemidemisemiquaver. British term for a sixty-fourth note.

Hillbilly Music. A description used for American country music, particularly that cultivated by the rustic inhabitants of the hill country of Kentucky.

Homophony. A style of composition based on chords, with the melody on top, as distinguished from Polyphony, in which all parts are contrapuntally active.

Horn. *see* French Horn. The colloquial use of the word horn for the trumpet is misleading.

Hornpipe. A rapid English sailor dance.

Hot Jazz. A term widely used during the swing era of jazz, and later paradoxically replaced by Cool Jazz.

Humoresque. A light, whimsical piece, usually for piano.

Hurdy-Gurdy. medieval string instrument operated with a crank that turns a rosined wheel which acts as a bow. It is often confused with the Barrel Organ, which has pipes.

Imitation. The repetition of a theme in another voice, in the same pitch, or in transposition, as applied in canons and fugues.

Impressionism. The style of composition associated with the French School of the first quarter of the twentieth century. Impressionism is programmatic in its esthetics, but its musical effect depends on subtle evocation rather than explicit tone painting. Its instrumentation exploits colorful nuances; its melodies and harmonies have an elusive, quasi-atonal quality.

Impromptu. The word suggests improvisation, but the Classical form of the instrumental impromptu (usually for piano) is actually a well-organized piece of music, symmetrically constructed, and subdivided into several contrasting sections.

Improvisation. A spontaneous performance on a solo instrument, usually piano or organ, often on a definite musical theme, thus approaching the form of a fantasy. Simultaneous improvisation by jazz groups (sometimes called jam sessions) is made possible by the use of certain prearranged routines and ingenious mutual adaptation.

Instrumentation. The art by which the instruments of the orchestra are blended or contrasted to achieve a desired effect.

Interlude. Literally, "between performances." A fairly prolonged composition between two sections of the principal work, either for a solo instrument or for an ensemble.

Intermezzo. An intermediate orchestral episode in an opera, practically synonymous with an interlude. The term is also applied to a composition for a solo instrument as a self-contained piece.

Interval. The distance between two notes.

Introduction. The initial section of a piece of music, often containing ornamental features, such as cadenzas.

Invention. Literally, "a finding." In the musical sense, an instrumental piece abounding in ingenious contrapuntal devices.

Inversion. An upside-down switch in the position of the notes in an interval, a chord, or a theme or melody.

Jazz. Universally popular type of modern American music, which in its numerous manifestations and reincarnations conveys an almost animal sense of exhilaration, accomplished by constant syncopation and dissonant harmony (in hot jazz, cool jazz, and swing), or else affecting a hypnotically monotonous beat.

Jig. A lively dance, usually in 6/8 time, similar to a hornpipe.

K. The initial letter of Köchel, the Austrian scholar who compiled the first comprehensive, chronological Mozart catalogue. K. is used as a symbol to identify by number each of Mozart's works.

Kettledrums. Pitched drums; in Classical orchestra scores, they are usually tuned to the tonic and the dominant of the principal key. Kettledrums are often referred to by their Italian name: Timpani.

Keyboard. A row of consecutive keys on the piano, organ, or other instruments on which keys are struck to produce musical tones.

Key Signature. A set of sharps or flats placed at the beginning of a piece after the clef, and each subsequent line, to indicate the principal key.

Klavier. The German word for Piano. In earlier times, the term, then often spelled Clavier, was applied to keyboard instruments in general (clavichord, harpsichord) and also to the manuals of the organ.

Konzertmeister. German for Concertmaster.

La. In Latin countries, and in Russia, the note A.

Lacrimoso. Tearful.

Lament. An elegy, or a funeral song.

Ländler. An Austrian country dance in triple time; precursor of the waltz.

Languido. Languid.

Larghetto. Literally, "a little *Largo.*" A tempo a little faster than *Largo.*

Largo. Broadly; a very slow tempo; performed in a deliberate, slow time.

Leading Tone. The seventh note of a scale, requiring resolution to the tonic.

Legato. Literally, "tied." The term indicates a smooth connection between melodic notes. *Legatissimo* means extremely *legato.*

Leggiero. With light ease; in nimble motion.

Legno. "Wood;" used in the expression mark *col legno,* a directive for a string instrumentalist to play with the back (wood) of the bow.

Leitmotiv. A leading motive in Wagner's music dramas, Richard Strauss's tone poems, and other works; a recognizable, recurrent motive, varying in tempo, dynamics, and sometimes in rhythm, that identifies a personage, object, or mood alluded to in the music.

Lento. Slow.

L.H. Abbreviation for Left Hand.

Libretto. Literally, "little book." A scenario, with a text, in operas, music dramas, and sometimes in ballets.

Lied. Strictly speaking, a song, any song; but in musical terminology, Lied applies specifically to a German art song for voice and piano.

Lieder. The plural of Lied.

Lieder ohne Worte. "Songs without Words;" songful pieces for piano solo, usually composed in song form. The title originated with the famous piano pieces by Mendelssohn.

Light Opera. Operetta, as distinct from *opera seria* or *opera semiseria.*

L'istesso Tempo. The same tempo as in the preceding section; a caution not to change the pace.

Loco. Literally, "place." A directive to return to the pitch as written, after a passage marked either 8········· or 8········

Lunga. Long; usually referring to a *fermata;* a pause or a hold.

Lusingando. Coaxing, ingratiating, seductive.

Lute. An old string instrument popular in Shakespearean times. It has a pear-shaped body with the neck turned back at a right angle; the strings are plucked with fingers. As in the guitar, it has frets to indicate the position of notes to be played, and its notation was usually in tablature. The large lute, Theorbo, has a separate set of permanently tuned strings that vibrate along with the plucked ones to increase the resonance. There were many varieties of lutes, of which the mandolin retains its popularity. Regular lutes are also being revived.

Lyric. Expressive, poetic. Lyric drama is a synonym for opera; the lyric stage is the opera theater.

Lyrics. Colloquial term for the text of a popular song or of a musical.

Madrigal. A non-religious vocal composition for solo or small chorus to words in the language of the country.

Madrigals were particularly popular in Italy during the Renaissance. By extension, a madrigal is an amorous song or an ode offered to an object of adoration.

Maestoso. In a stately, majestic manner.

Maestro. Literally, "a master." A term commonly used in Italy, Russia, and other countries to address conductors or composers.

Maggiore. Italian word for major tonality. The word indicating a major-key section in a piece written in a minor key with the same tonic.

Major Key. A tonality based on a major scale consisting, consecutively and upwards, of two whole-steps, one half-step, three whole-steps, and one half-step.

Major Triad. A triad consisting of the tonic, the mediant, and the dominant of a major scale, as C, E, G in the C-major scale.

Mandolin. A pear-shaped string instrument which is plucked with a plectrum and often used to accompany serenades.

Manual. A hand keyboard (as against the pedal or "foot" keyboard). While most keyboard instruments have only one manual [keyboard], organs generally have more than one manual and a pedal.

Maracas. A Latin American shaker made out of a gourd with pellets inside.

Marcato. "Marked, emphasized." In phrases like *marcato il tenore, marcato il basso*, etc., the instruction to bring out the tenor, the bass, or another indicated voice. *Marcata la melodia* often occurs when the composer wants the melody, in an inner voice or in the bass, to be brought out.

March. A piece of music in 4/4 or 2/4 time and occasionally in 6/8.

Marcia. "March;" used in the tempo mark *alla marcia* (like a march).

Marcia funebre. Funeral march.

Marimba. Percussion instrument of Latin American or African origin, consisting of large wooden bars which are struck with sticks.

Martellato. "Hammer-like;" applied to a percussive articulation of rapid passages on the piano.

Marziale. In a martial fashion; march-like.

Mass. The principal and most solemn service of the Roman Catholic Church. It consists of the following parts: Kyrie, Gloria, Credo, Sanctus, Benedictus, and Agnus Dei. In modern times, Masses have been composed to popular texts, and even in jazz and rock style.

Mässig. Moderately; deliberately.

Mazurka. A popular Polish dance in syncopated 3/4 time.

Measure. A metrical division between two barlines; a bar indicating the number of beats.

Mediant. The third note of the major or minor scale; the middle note of a tonic triad.

Meno. "Less;" used in such connections as *meno mosso* (less quickly).

Menuet. French, as well as German, for minuet.

Mesto. Mournful; wistful.

Meter. The number of units in a bar.

Metronome. A pendulum-like device to measure time.

The letters "M.M." stand for Maelzel's Metronome. The duration of a given note is indicated by the number of beats per minute. Thus, M.M. 60 means sixty beats per minute, or one beat per second; M.M. 120 means 120 beats per minute, or two per second, etc. Today, the M.M. is usually dropped in favor of the beat unit: ♩ = 60 means 60 quarter beats per minute.

Mezzo forte. Medium loud. Abbreviated *mf*.

Mezzo piano. Medium soft. Abbreviated *mp*.

Mezzo Soprano. Literally, "Middle Soprano;" the female voice lower than soprano but higher than alto.

mf. Abbreviation for *mezzo forte*.

Mi. In Latin countries, and in Russia, the note E.

Middle C. The note situated four octaves down from the highest note of the modern piano keyboard and three octaves and a minor third higher than the lowest note on the keyboard; the C closest to the middle of the keyboard.

Military Band. An instrumental group containing only wind and percussion instruments.

Minore. Italian word for minor tonality. The word is used to indicate a minor-key section in a piece written in a major key with the same tonic.

Minor Key. A tonality based on a minor scale. This scale has three different forms: 1) the harmonic minor scale, consisting, consecutively and upwards, of one whole-step, one half-step, two whole-steps, one half-step, one and a half steps, and one half-step; 2) the natural minor scale: one whole-step, one half-step, two whole-steps, one half-step, two whole-steps; 3) the melodic minor scale: one whole-step, one half-step, four whole-steps, one half-step.

Minor Triad. A triad consisting of the tonic, mediant, and dominant of a minor scale, as in C, E-flat, G in the C-minor scale.

Minuet. A French court dance in a moderate 3/4 time. It is in Ternary Form, in which the initial section is repeated at the end. The middle section is called a Trio, because in early Minuets it was usually performed by three instruments. A Minuet is often included in the Baroque suite. It also serves as the third movement between the slow second movement and the finale of the Classical symphony and string quartet.

Misterioso. Mysterious.

Moderato. Moderate, as in *Molto moderato*, in a very moderate tempo.

Modern Music. General description of music composed since 1900. In colloquial parlance, modern music covers the entire field of popular songs, musicals, jazz, etc.

Modes. Diatonic progressions that differ from one another by the order of whole tones and semitones. If played on the white keys of the piano, the mode from D to D is called Dorian; E to E, Phrygian; F to F, Lydian; G to G, Mixolydian; A to A, Aeolian; and B to B, Locrian (very rarely used). The C-major scale, i.e., C to C, corresponds to the Ionian mode. The modes originated with medieval church music and continued to underlie all Western music through the seventeenth century, when they were gradually succeeded by major and minor. Many twentieth-century composers have revived them in their music.

Modulation. Smooth transition from one key to another according to set rules.

Moll. German term for minor, as in *C moll* (C minor).

Molto. "Much; very;" as in *Molto allegro* (very fast), *Molto adagio* (very slow).

Moment Musical. A brief piano piece popularized by Schubert, and portraying a passing musical inspiration.

Moog. A keyboard-operated electronic synthesizer of sounds, invented and named after the American engineer Robert Moog.

Morceau. A short piece of instrumental music.

Mordent. An ornament used in Baroque music, indicating a short, quick downward trill, as in C-B-C.

Morendo. Dying away.

Mosso. Moving along.

Motet. A historically significant form of polyphonic vocal music, which flourished during the Middle Ages. In strict application, a motet is a choral work of a contrapuntal nature to a sacred text in Latin.

Motive. A short theme, usually of episodic nature. See also *Leitmotiv*.

Moto. "Motion or movement," as in *Andante con moto* (moving along).

Moto perpetuo. Perpetual motion.

Mouth Organ. A set of reeds in a frame, giving out a scale and played by blowing into it. Also called Harmonica.

Mouvement. Movement.

Movimento. Movement.

mp. Abbreviation for *mezzo piano*.

Musette. A French bagpipe with a constantly sounding tone on the tonic, dominant, or both. Also the middle section of a gavotte with a drone bass imitative of a bagpipe.

Musical. A colloquial term for a musical comedy.

Musical Comedy. A genre of American operetta, with spoken dialogue and singing in about equal measure.

Musicology. The science of music. The concept includes all branches of music—theory, history, esthetics, lexicography, bibliography, etc.

Mute. A device used to soften the tone of an instrument, as a damper with prongs placed on the bridge of a string instrument, or a wooden cone inserted into the bell of a brass instrument, or even a hat placed over the bell of a wind instrument (in jazz bands).

Nachtmusik. German for serenade (literally, "Night Music"). Mozart's "Eine kleine Nachtmusik" is "A Little Serenade."

Nachtstück. A nocturne.

Natural. A note played at its basic pitch, neither sharp nor flat.

Niente. "Nothing;" used in the expression mark *quasi niente* (almost nothing) to indicate an extreme attenuation of the sound.

Nocturne. A characteristic piece for piano, set in a nocturnal romantic mood, poetically popularized by Chopin. It is usually in a three-part form, with the main theme returning at the end. It corresponds to the German Romantic form *Nachtstück*.

Noël. French word for Christmas; any popular Christmas song or carol.

Non. "Not," as in *non legato* (not connected), *non troppo* (not too much).

Nonet. A work for nine players.

Non-Tempered Scale. The natural scale based on the overtone series, in which enharmonic notes may differ from one another, so that C-sharp would be slightly sharper than D-flat, etc.

Notation. A method of writing down music, either by placing notes, etc., on staves to indicate pitches and durations, etc., or by writing numbers, etc., to indicate the positions of fingers on an instrument. The latter form of notation is called Tablature (Lute Tablature, Organ Tablature, etc.) and is hardly ever used any longer. In ultra-modern music, various symbols are used to indicate such effects as the highest possible note playable on a given instrument, tone-clusters, tapping on the body of an instrument, quarter tones, etc. Another notational trend of today's avant-garde is often called "graphic notation." Here the composer draws imaginative lines and shapes, to be interpreted freely by the performer(s).

Novelette. A short piece of a romantic nature, usually for piano; the name is derived from the literary form novella, a little novel.

Nuance. A delicate shade of expression; a slight permissible modification of tempo, rhythm, or dynamics.

Obbligato. Literally, "obligatory." The term indicates that a certain instrument is essential, as in *violino obbligato*, and it is the opposite of *ad libitum*. Paradoxically, an inversion of meanings occurred, and *obbligato* has come to mean *not* obligatory, but optional, particularly in modern pieces.

Oboe. A woodwind instrument with a somewhat nasal, penetrating tone. Its range is about two octaves and a half, beginning on B-flat below middle C. The Oboe d'amore, a once popular instrument, is pitched a minor third below the oboe. The English Horn belongs to the oboe family and has a compass of a little over two octaves; the lowest note is E below middle C. The Bass Oboe, or Heckelphone, is sometimes used in modern scores.

Ocarina. An egg-shaped, small wind instrument which can produce only a few high-pitched notes and is sometimes used for special effects or as a toy.

Octave. The basic interval of eight diatonic degrees; it completes the scale.

Octet. A composition for eight players.

Ode. A work of a solemn nature, usually for voices.

Opera. A musical stage work, generally sung throughout, involving soloists, chorus, and orchestra, and often including ballet interludes. In concert performances, opera is given without theatrical paraphernalia. Wagner preferred to call his operas Music Dramas.

Opera buffa. Literally, "a buffoon opera," that is, an opera with a comic libretto.

Opéra comique. *see* Comic Opera.

Opera semiseria. A serious opera containing comic elements.

Opera seria. Serious opera, as opposed to light opera.

Operetta. "Little opera;" usually gently comical in character, as opposed to *opera seria*, serious opera.

Opus. Literally, "work;" a musical composition.

Opus Number. The number assigned for chronological identification to a composition or a group of works of a particular composer.

Oratorio. A work for chorus and soloists, accompanied by an instrumental ensemble, usually of a religious nature and of considerable length.

Orchestra. An ensemble of instrumental players. Depending on its character, it may be described as a symphony orchestra, a chamber orchestra, a string orchestra, or a theater orchestra, etc.

Orff Instruments. A percussion ensemble devised by the German composer Carl Orff for educational purposes, containing traditional drums, as well as exotic instruments such as Maracas, Bongo Drums, and others, many in simplified versions.

Organ (Pipe Organ). A keyboard instrument usually having several manuals and a set of pedals (very large white and black keys arranged like an ordinary keyboard but played by the player's feet). The sound is produced by a stream of air blown through the pipes. The manuals and pedals operate a number of so-called "stops" capable of generating a variety of tone colors and overtones. Many stops are named after the wind instruments whose tone colors are imitated; but there are also stops with such imaginative names as *Voix céleste* (heavenly voice). To obtain maximum sonority, the organist pulls out all the stops. *See also* Baroque Organ. Some modern electronic (theater) organs are structures of impressive proportions, capable of filling a hall with brilliant sound.

Organ Point. A sustained bass, usually the tonic or the dominant of the principal key of a piece, or both simultaneously.

Ornamentation. The practice of melodic embellishment by means of trills, mordents, grace notes, appoggiaturas, etc.

Ostinato. Literally, "obstinate;" a recurrent theme, usually in the bass, with contrapuntal voices in the upper registers (*see also* Basso Ostinato).

Overtones. Barely audible sounds which in pianos and other string instruments are produced by the secondary vibrations of a string that naturally divides into two, three, four, etc., sections. Overtones can be heard by selective attention. The lowest and strongest overtone is an octave above the fundamental; the next, a twelfth (octave plus a fifth), followed by two octaves, two octaves plus a major third, etc., theoretically ad infinitum. In wind instruments, the air column acts like a string in a string instrument, but the shape of the instrument's bore (cylindrical, conical, etc.) adds complexities not present in string-generated overtones. The tone color of an instrument is determined by the proportionate strength of its overtones.

Overture. Literally, "an opening." Its most common form is an orchestral introduction to an opera, containing its principal themes or leading motives; by extension, any orchestral work that suggests a definite literary, national, historic, or emotional subject.

p. Abbreviation for *piano* (soft).

Panpipes. A set of pipes of different pitches, made of hollow reeds, and attached to each other; associated with the Greek god Pan.

Parlando. "Speaking;" singing in a half-spoken manner, particularly in a recitative.

Parlor Organ. *see* Reed Organ.

Part. An individual voice in a polyphonic composition; sheet music for a particular instrument, as in violin part, flute part, etc.

Partials. *see* Overtones.

Partita. An instrumental suite.

Part Song. Originally, a type of polyphonic song, with several parts participating on an equal basis; later, the term applied chiefly to a vocal composition, with the melody accompanied by an instrumental ensemble.

Passacaglia. Baroque type of contrapuntally constructed movement in which a sharply defined subject is repeated throughout, usually in the bass.

Passage. A brief episode of a composition; a transition. Passage work means a display of virtuosity by an instrumentalist.

Passing Note. A dissonant note passing between two harmony notes.

Passion. A religious work for voices with or without instrumental accompaniment, descriptive of the Crucifixion, and set in a dramatic form.

Pastorale. A short instrumental or vocal composition of a pastoral nature, suggesting a scene of poetic rustic life.

Pathétique. Full of pathos; highly impassioned and emotional.

Pavane. A stately court dance, popular in Europe in the sixteenth century. Several modern compositions entitled Pavane imitate the movement if not the essence of this dance. The spelling Pavanne is erroneous.

Pedal. Literally, "pertaining to the foot." In pianos there are three pedals: the loud pedal, which releases the dampers over the strings to create rich resonance; the soft pedal, which shifts the keyboard, causing the hammers to strike only one string (marked in the music *una corda*, "one string"), but which in upright pianos merely brings the hammers closer to the strings to effect a softer sound; and the sustaining pedal in the middle, which releases the dampers of only the notes that are pressed down. In organ playing, the pedal is an extra keyboard and thus a melody device; master organists are as agile with their feet as with their hands. In the harp, the pedal raises or lowers the pitch.

Percussion. A class of instruments vibrated by striking.

The traditional percussion instruments are Kettledrums, or Timpani, Bass Drum, Snare Drum, Cymbals, Triangle, Tambourine, and Gong. To these should be added the more special Bongo Drums, Maracas (shaker), Claves (wooden sticks), Guiros (scratchers), and Woodblocks.

Perdendosi. Literally, "losing itself;" an indication to play softer and softer to the point of bare audibility.

Perfect Pitch. *see* Absolute Pitch.

Period. A musical phrase with well-defined limits.

Pesante. Ponderous; heavy.

Phrase. Any short melodic section.

Phrasing. Fashioning a phrase; performing a melody gracefully and with taste.

Piacere. *see* A piacere.

Piacevole. Pleasingly.

Pianissimo. Very soft. Abbreviated *pp*.

Pianississimo. Very, very soft. Abbreviated *ppp*.

Piano. Soft. Abbreviated *p*.

Piano. The most common musical keyboard instrument in the home. Its original name was *gravicembalo col piano e forte* ("a harpsichord with soft and loud"), that is, an instrument capable of producing different gradations of softness and loudness through key pressure.

Pianoforte. Literally, "soft-loud;" an early name of the piano.

Piano Quartet. A work for piano and three instruments (usually violin, viola, and cello).

Piano Quintet. A work for piano and string quartet or any other combination of four more instruments.

Piano Score. An arrangement of an orchestral work for piano.

Piano Trio. A composition for piano, violin, and cello.

Piccolo. "Little." The highest wind instrument; a small flute one octave higher than the regular flute, with a range of nearly three octaves, reaching the highest C within the audible range.

Pitch. The height of a tone, usually determined by the accepted frequency of vibrations of middle A (440 vibrations are regarded as standard pitch for A).

Più. "More;" used in such expressions as *più mosso* (more movement).

Pizz. Abbreviation for *pizzicato*.

Pizzicato. "Pinched;" a directive to a string instrument player to pluck the strings with the fingers.

Plainchant. Liturgical music, sung in unison, without harmonization or accompaniment, usually in free, proselike rhythms.

Player Piano. A mechanical piano in which the hammers are usually set in motion by streams of air pushed through the holes in a roll of perforated paper and thus activating the instrument's mechanism.

Plus. French word for "more;" as in *plus animé* (more animation) and *plus lentement* (more slowly).

Pochissimo. Very little; a tiny bit.

Poco. "A little;" *poco a poco* (little by little). Also used to modify the expression marks, as in *poco ritardando* (slowing down a little); *poco crescendo* (a little louder); *poco animato* (a little animated).

Poi. "Then;" used in phrases such as *Da capo e poi la coda* (from the beginning and then the coda).

Polka. A lively dance in 2/4 time, originated not in Poland but in Bohemia.

Polonaise. The French word for "Polish." The Polonaise is a Polish national dance in 3/4 time in a deliberate, measured tempo.

Polyphony. A contrapuntal technique which reached its flowering in the Renaissance and the Baroque periods and which involves the composition of several melodic strands intertwining in an elaborate texture. Polyphony, which literally means "many-voicedness," is graphically described as a linear or horizontal type of musical texture, as opposed to homophony which exploits vertical harmonic combinations.

Polytonality. Simultaneous use of two or more different tonalities; playing in different keys. In much modern music polytonality has become a standard technique.

Pomposo. Pompous.

Ponticello. Literally, "a small bridge;" used in the indication for string instruments: *sul ponticello*, meaning to play on the bridge, or as close as possible to the bridge, producing a nasal effect.

Pop Music. A colloquial description of popular American music in its most informal vein.

Portative. A pipe organ small enough to be movable.

pp. Abbreviation for *pianissimo* (very soft).

ppp. Abbreviation for *pianississimo* (very, very soft).

Prelude. A rather short piece of instrumental music of an introductory nature. In actual composition, preludes outgrew this technical definition and assumed the character of independent instrumental works. In operatic works, Prelude is used occasionally instead of Overture (for example, in Wagner's opera *Tristan und Isolde*).

Prestissimo. The superlative of *Presto*; very, very fast.

Presto. Very fast.

Prima Donna. "First lady;" the leading soprano in an opera.

Primo. "First;" used in expressions such as *tempo primo* (the same tempo as at first). *Primo* also refers to the upper part in pieces for piano four-hands (the lower part is marked *Secondo*).

Program Music. Descriptive music suggesting a landscape, a mood, a romantic scene, or containing an allusion to a literary or artistic work.

Psalm. A hymn; a sacred song.

Quadrille. A ballroom square-dance popular in the nineteenth century.

Quarter-Tone. Half a semitone; an interval which can be performed accurately only on electronic instruments, but is sometimes used as a passing tone in modern compositions.

Quartet. A composition for four performers.

Quasi. "Almost;" used in such expressions as *quasi niente* (almost nothing); *quasi presto* (almost fast); *quasi una fantasia* (almost a fantasy).

Quasi niente. "Almost nothing;" indicating an extreme *decrescendo*.

Quaver. British word for an eighth-note.

Quintet. A composition for five performers.

Ragtime. An early type of American popular music, marked by vigorous syncopation on the off-beat in 4/4 time.

Rallentando. Gradually becoming slower.

Re. In Latin countries, and in Russia, the note D.

Recapitulation. A return of the initial section of a movement in sonata form.

Recital. A solo concert by an instrumentalist or a vocalist.

Recitative. Half-recited, half-sung portion in an opera, accompanied by a series of chords.

Recorder. A vertical, wooden flute, popular in the Renaissance and Baroque eras, and again in our time. It is built in different sizes: sopranino (or high soprano); soprano (also known as descant); alto (or treble); tenor; and bass.

Reed Organ. In the Middle Ages and the Renaissance, a small, portable organ whose sounds were produced exclusively by small, rather strident reeds. It was called a Regal.—Since the nineteenth century, a parlor organ, or harmonium, with one or two keyboards, and occasionally also a pedal keyboard. Its tones are produced by an air stream that causes metal tongues to vibrate. The air is pumped by pedals; the volume is controlled by the air pressure.

Refrain. A recurrent portion of a song at the end of each stanza.

Regal. *see* Reed Organ.

Relative Keys. Different keys with the same key signature, such as C major and A minor (no flats, no sharps); or D-flat major and B-flat minor (five flats).

Reprise. A return of a section in a formal composition, such as a sonata; recapitulation. Also used in musical comedy for repeats with full ensemble.

Requiem. The Mass for the dead, which opens with the Latin word *Requiem* (rest, peace).

Resolution. The process by which a dissonance or a dissonant chord is followed by a consonance, or by which a melodic appoggiatura passes to the harmonic note.

Rest. A sign for silence for a specified number of beats.

Retrograde. A term applied to a theme played backwards, from the last note to the first. It is also known as a crab movement (although crabs actually move sideways, not backwards).

R.H. Abbreviation for Right Hand.

Rhapsody. An instrumental work in free form with contrasting themes alternating in improvisatory succession.

Rhythm. A pattern of durations (note-values).

Rinforzando. "Reinforcing." The same as *sforzando.*

Risoluto. Resolute.

Rit. Abbreviation for *ritardando.*

Ritardando. Gradually getting slower.

Ritenuto. Holding back the tempo; practically the same as *ritardando.*

Ritmico. Rhythmically.

Ritornello. A refrain; a constantly recurring episode, though sometimes varied in harmony and rhythm.

Rock 'n' Roll. Modern type of original American popular music, characterized by a steady beat, almost invariably arranged in 4/4 time, and a ballad-like singing recitation, accompanied by electric guitars, drums, and piano or electronic organ, among others, and often reaching the utmost degree of loudness, with human voices expanding into shrieks and the sound further amplified and sometimes distorted by electronic devices.

Romance. A short composition in a slow tempo, either for voice or for a solo instrument.

Romantic Music. The style of composition which flourished in the nineteenth century, characterized by programmatic representation of nature and emotions.

Rondeau. The French term for rondo.

Rondo. A musical form in which the principal theme recurs periodically, in alternation with contrasting sections.

Round. A perpetual canon.

Rubato. An expressive manner of interpretation; *tempo rubato* suggests rhythmic freedom within strict time. The word rubato actually means "robbed."

Rumba. A Cuban dance in a highly syncopated rhythm.

Samba. A vivacious Brazilian dance in 2/4 time, marked by a vigorous rhythmic beat.

Sarabande. A stately court dance in 3/2 time with the stress on the second beat; often included in the Baroque suite.

Sarrusophone. A large brass instrument in the bass range, invented by the French bandmaster Sarrus, and used in military bands to replace the Double-Bassoon.

Saxophone. A transposing instrument whose name is derived from its inventor, Adolphe Sax. Depending on size and range, Saxophones are designated as sopranino, soprano, alto, tenor, baritone, bass, and contrabass, with a compass of two and a half octaves; they are tuned in B-flat or E-flat. The Saxophone is the chief melody instrument of the jazz band.

Scale. A progression of notes, following the diatonic, chromatic, or some other order of intervals.

Scherzando. Like a scherzo; a passage to be played in the light spirit of a scherzo.

Scherzo. Literally, "a jest." A lively movement in 3/4 time, in a strict, symmetric form, often inserted in a sonata or symphony in place of the traditional minuet; also an instrumental piece of music, especially for piano.

Score. The graphic (written) form of a musical work for several orchestral and/or vocal parts, with staves one under another to give a synopsis of all participating components, for use by the conductor or student. Also called Full Score. A small-size edition of a Full Score is called a Study Score or Pocket Score.

Secco. "Dry." In conjunction with the recitative, the term indicates a certain dryness of accompaniment. *Recitativo secco* is accompanied only by chords.

Secondo. The lower part in pieces for piano four-hands (the upper part is marked *Primo*).

Segno. "Sign;" used in such expressions as *Dal segno al fine* (from the sign to the finish).

Segue. Literally, "it follows." A term to indicate "following through," going over immediately to the next section.

Seguidilla. A vivacious Spanish dance in 3/4 time.

Semiquaver. British term for a half-quaver; a sixteenth-note. It is equal to two demisemiquavers and four hemidemisemiquavers.

Semitone. A half-step; a chromatic interval.

Semplice. Simple; without affectation.

Sempre. Always, throughout; as in *sempre accelerando* (always accelerating).

Senza. "Without;" used in such phrases as *senza rigore* (without rigor, freely), *senza sordini* (without mutes), or *senza pedale* (without pedals).

Septet. A composition for seven performers.

Sequence. An important melodic resource in which a phrase is repeated several times, each time one or more degrees higher or lower. If it progresses along the scale degrees of the tonality of the piece, its intervals will change according to its position in the scale, and it is called a *tonal* sequence; if it retains its original interval structure, it is called a *real* sequence, but it will no longer fit the scale and will therefore modulate to other tonalities.

Serenade. Literally, "an evening song." In Classical usage, the term applies to any instrumental or vocal composition of a light and harmonious nature.

Serenata. Italian for serenade.

Seria. Serious. The term is used especially in the designation *opera seria*, serious opera, as opposed to *opera buffa*, or comic opera.

Set Piece. In an opera, a separate scene of a fairly strict formal nature, often unrelated to the rest of the production.

Sextet. A composition for six performers.

Sforzando. Reinforcing one particular note or chord; abbreviated, *sf* or *sfz*.

Sharp. A sign indicating the raising of a pitch by a semitone (half-step).

Sheet Music. Printed music on unbound sheets.

Siciliana. A slow instrumental piece or a song, derived from the folk rhythms of Sicily, and set in a minor mode, in 6/8 time.

Sight Reading. Playing or singing an unfamiliar piece of music at first sight. Also called in Italian, *a prima vista*.

Simile. Similarly; a directive to apply phrasing and dynamics similar to the preceding section.

Sinfonia. The Classical term for a movement in a symphonic form, now applied often to suggest the Baroque character of a modern composition.

Sinfonietta. "A little symphony." A relatively short work for a small orchestral or chamber group.

Sing-Song. Singing in a monotonous and repetitive manner.

Singspiel. A light opera containing spoken dialogue, usually in the vernacular.

Slentando. Getting slower and more languid in expression.

Slur. A curved line indicating that the notes so joined should be played *legato*. In a vocal part, a slur indicates that the grouped notes are to be sung in one breath.

Smorzando. Softening in tone and nuances.

Soft Pedal. The left pedal on the piano, which shifts the keyboard so that the hammers strike only a single string. (In upright pianos the hammers are merely brought closer to the strings to effect a softer sound.)

Sognando. Dreamily.

Sol. In Latin countries, and in Russia, the note G.

Solenne. Solemnly.

Solfeggio. Practice of vocal exercises, specifically for ear training and sight reading.

Solo. Literally, "single." A piece of music for a single performer, with or without accompaniment. Also a solo passage within a non-solo work.

Soloist. A solo performer, either with or without accompaniment.

Sonata. The literal meaning of the word is "sounded," as opposed to *cantata*, "sung." The sonata is the all-pervading type of instrumental music of the Classical period. In its most developed form it contains four movements. In most sonatas it is the first movement that is, properly speaking, cast in "sonata form," containing two contrasting subjects; the second movement is usually a slow theme with variations; the third is a minuet or a scherzo, and the last, the finale, is a rondo or a rondo-sonata, a form that partakes of elements characteristic of both rondo and sonata. Such is the scheme; in actual practice, the composition of sonatas fills its outline with great freedom of invention and choice.

Sonatina. "A little sonata." It follows the general scheme of the sonata, but may have fewer movements, and be of a lighter character.

Song. A short vocal composition, either accompanied or unaccompanied. The frequent usage of the word "song" for an instrumental work without a singing part is erroneous and regrettable.

Song Form. The term is usually applied to a *da capo* form in which the initial section is repeated. An instrumental composition is said to be in song form if the *da capo* specification is observed.

Sopra. "Above;" often used to indicate which hand is placed above the other in passages played with cross-hands, as in *mano destra sopra* (right hand above), or *mano sinistra sopra* (left hand above).

Soprano. The highest female voice.

Sordino. A mute; *con sordini* in string-instrument parts means "with mutes;" *senza sordini* ("without mutes") is a directive to take off the mutes. In piano music, *sordini* is an indication to use the soft pedal.

Sostenuto. Sustained, yet played without changes of tempo.

Sotto voce. Literally, "under the voice;" a term indicating very soft singing, often for dramatic effect.

Soul Singing. A style of Negro Gospel singing, marked with great expressive force, and associated with the social movement of black protest.

Sousaphone. A spiral type of Bass Tuba, which is coiled

around the player, with a large shallow bell turned forwards. The Sousaphone is named after Sousa, the March King, who used it often in his bands.

Spinet. A keyboard instrument smaller than the standard upright piano; in earlier times, a small harpsichord.

Spiritual. A religious song, especially the genre created by Negro slaves in the South.

Square Dance. A parlor or country dance, such as a quadrille, danced by several couples in a square formation.

Square Time. A popular term for 4/4 time; march time.

Staccato. Performing in detached, skipping notes; indicated by dots above the notes. *Staccatissimo* is the extreme application of *staccato*, with each note barely touched and immediately released.

Ständchen. A German word for a serenade.

Stanza. A symmetric unit of a song.

Stretto. Literally, "pulled together;" a term indicating a certain hastening of the movement. In a fugue, *stretto* means closer overlapping of voices, usually occurring at the end and leading to the coda.

String Bass. A colloquial term for Double-Bass.

Stringendo. Stringing in; growing more intense; increasing the tempo and the dynamics.

String Quartet. An ensemble comprised of two violins, viola, and cello; a composition for such an ensemble, usually in sonata form.

Studio Piano. A small Upright Piano.

Study. An etude; a technical exercise.

Subdominant. The fourth note of a scale.

Subito. Immediately; suddenly. *Subito piano* means play soft immediately; *attacca subito*, start the next section without a break.

Subject. A theme; the principal statement in a fugue.

Submediant. The sixth note of a scale.

Suite. A group of movements, unified by a common stylistic manner. The Baroque suite consists of dance forms, arranged in a contrasting order.

Supertonic. The second degree of the scale.

Sustaining Pedal. The middle pedal on the piano, enabling the player to sustain a single note or chord.

Swing. A smooth, sophisticated style of jazz playing, popular in the 1930's and often involving a rather large band.

Symphonic Poem. An orchestral work that follows a literary or pictorial idea. Also called Tone Poem.

Symphony. An extensive work scored for a full orchestra, traditionally in four movements and in sonata form, with the two outer movements in rapid tempo, a slow second movement, and a minuet or scherzo for the third movement. Modern symphonies are often cast in a single movement, diversified to include the contrasting elements inherent in sonata form. Exceptionally, a symphony may include vocal parts, the most famous example being Beethoven's Ninth Symphony with its choral finale.

Symphony Orchestra. A full orchestra capable of performing classical and modern repertory.

Syncopation. Cross rhythms, produced by accents on the secondary beats in the measure; a powerful device, importantly used in Baroque music, as well as by Beethoven, Brahms, and many others. Syncopation is the rhythmic essence of ragtime and jazz.

Synthesizer. *see* Electronic Music.

Tablature. A system of notation indicating the position of the fingers on an instrument, rather than the pitches to be sounded. It is now obsolete, except for the ukelele and the guitar.

Tacet. Literally, "it is silent." Traditional term to indicate a bar of rest when the entire orchestra is silent, or to indicate that an instrument belonging to the total orchestration remains silent throughout an entire movement or section.

Tamtam. A metal-disk instrument similar to, but not identical with a Gong. (It lacks the gong's center elevation, or "dome".)

Tango. Syncopated Argentinian dance in 2/4 time, similar in rhythm to the Habanera.

Tarantella. A quick Italian dance in 6/8 time. The name of the dance comes from the southern Italian town of Taranto; the legend had it that dancing the tarantella was a cure for the bite of the tarantula, a large poisonous spider prevalent in Taranto.

Tempered Scale. A scale in which the twelve chromatic half-steps are tuned to be equidistant, making it possible to transpose any music into any of the twelve major and minor keys without distorting the component intervals. Also called Well-Tempered Scale.

Tempo. Time; pace; speed. The tempo is indicated either by the Metronome mark or by Italian words, such as *Largo, Andante, Allegro, Presto,* etc.

Tempo di Marcia. March time.

Tempo giusto. Precise tempo.

Tempo primo. First tempo; the same speed as at first.

Tenor. High male voice; also, a tenor trombone or tenor saxophone for short.

Tenor Clef. C-clef, used in cello and bassoon parts; it indicates the position of middle C on the fourth line of the staff.

Tenuto. Sustained; without diminishing in strength.

Ternary Form. A symmetrical musical construction consisting of three sections, of which the first and the third are either completely identical or recognizably similar. The second section, based on a contrasting theme, is usually set in the key of the dominant or subdominant. Ternary Form is often called Song Form because art songs, particularly the German Lieder, are in clear ternary form. The Minuet and the Scherzo are examples of ternary form. The form of the typical sonata movement is ternary, with the Exposition and the Recapitulation being the outer sections and the Development the middle section.

Tessitura. Italian word for texture; it indicates the most effective range of a voice.

Tetrachord. A group of four consecutive notes in a major or minor scale; the initial four notes from the tonic to the subdominant form the lower tetrachord; the four notes from the dominant to the upper tonic form the upper tetrachord.

Theater Arrangement. A transcription of an orchestral work or an opera for a reduced ensemble, so that it can be performed by small groups. Theater arrangements usually have cues for more common instruments to fill in for those that cannot be obtained for a particular performance. The piano fills in the harmonies.

Theme. The principal melody or motive in a musical composition.

Theme and Variations. A form of composition in which the principal theme is clearly and explicitly stated at the beginning, and is then followed by a number of variations.

Theme Song. The most prominent song in a musical, or a movie, calculated to express the abiding sentiment of the entire production.

Theorbo. A large Lute.

Tie. A curved line between two adjacent notes of the same pitch, to indicate that the note must be held, without new attack, for the total duration of the sum of the note-values tied.

Timbre. Tone color.

Time Signature. Indicator of the number of beats in a measure, designated by a fraction, with the denominator in powers of 2 (2, 4, 8, 16, 32, etc.) showing note-values (half-notes, quarter-notes, eighth-notes), and the numerator showing the number of such units in a bar, as in 3/2 (three half-notes to a bar), 5/8 (five eighth-notes to a bar), etc.

Timpani. Kettledrums.

Toccata. Literally, "touched." A composition for a keyboard instrument, usually marked by rapid passages in uniform tempo.

Tom-tom. An Indian drum producing a dull but penetrating sound.

Tonality. A definite key, in major or minor, as opposed to the absence of a key in Atonality. The combination of several tonalities played simultaneously is called Polytonality.

Tone. Any clear musical sound.

Tone Color. Distinctive characteristic of the sound of a specific instrument.

Tone Poem. A symphonic poem.

Tone-Row. The principal theme in dodecaphonic (twelve-tone) music, consisting of twelve different notes.

Tonic. The first note of a scale.

tr. Abbreviation for trill.

Tranquillo. Tranquil, calm.

Transcription. An arrangement of a musical composition with a different instrumentation from the original, as of a symphony transcribed for piano or a piano piece transcribed for orchestra.

Transposing Instruments. Instruments (mostly wind instruments) which sound higher or lower than notated. Thus, Clarinets in B-flat, A, or E-flat produce these notes, respectively, when they play a written C. The French Horn usually is "in F:" when a written C is played, the Horn sounds the F below the C. English Horns are always in F and sound similarly. Trumpets are usually in B-flat; Saxophones in B-flat or E-flat. The Baritone is sometimes written in C (i.e., untransposed) or in B-flat. The Piccolo sounds one octave higher than written; the Double-Bass transposes one octave down. Instruments in C sound as written.

Transposition. Raising or lowering the pitch of a given composition, thereby changing its key, unless transposed an octave up or down.

Traps. Drums in a dance band.

Tre. Italian for three. Used in such connections as *a tre* (three instruments playing at the same time), *tre corde* (all three strings of a piano tone struck by the hammer, i.e., played without the soft pedal).

Treble. High register. The treble clef, or high-register clef, is the G-clef.

Tremolo. Literally, "trembling." On the piano, a quick alternation of tones farther apart than those of a trill; a "wide trill." In string instruments, a quick alternation of up and down bowing. Often used for dramatic effect.

Triad. A chord consisting of three notes, generally formed by the intervals of a third and a fifth above a given note. A major triad has a major third at the bottom and a minor third at the top, aggregating to a perfect fifth; a minor triad has a minor third at the bottom and a major third at the top; in a diminished triad, two minor thirds aggregate to a diminished fifth; in an augmented triad, two major thirds aggregate to an augmented fifth.

Trill. An embellishment in which the principal note alternates with the note above in rapid motion.

Trio. A composition for three instruments or voices. A String Trio is scored for violin, viola, and cello; a Woodwind Trio may include three identical or different wind instruments; a Piano Trio is scored for violin, cello, and piano. The term Trio is also applied to the middle section of a minuet, because it was traditionally scored for three instruments.

Trio Sonata. A Baroque form of composition written for two violins and cello, harmonically supported by a continuo instrument (*see* Continuo).

Triple Concerto. A concerto for three instruments with orchestra.

Triplet. A group of three notes of equal duration, in a metric context in which beats are normally divided by two, not three; the division into three notes of a note-value which normally divides into only two notes.

Tritone. A melodic interval of three whole-tones, as C up to F-sharp. Because the tritone does not occur in either major or minor tetrachords, medieval theorists regarded it as the "diabolus in musica," and prohibited its use in composition. But in the twentieth century the tritone has paradoxically become the cornerstone of atonality, dodecaphony, and other modern techniques.

Trombone. Literally, "big trumpet." It is a low brass instrument in which the pitch is changed by pulling a slide in and out, thus shortening or lengthening the total tube of the instrument. Also called Slide Trombone. The most frequent form is the Tenor Trombone with a range from E below the bass-clef staff to B-flat above middle C. The Bass Trombone is one fourth lower; the Double-Bass Trombone one octave lower.

Troppo. "Excessive." Used in expressions like *Allegro ma non troppo* (fast, but not too much so).

Trumpet. The brightest instrument of the brass choir; its range extends for nearly three octaves, from E below middle C to the high C. The B-flat Trumpet is most often used in traditional music. The C Trumpet is encountered in modern works; it sounds as written.

Tuba. The lowest instrument of the brass choir; also called Bass Tuba. Its compass extends from the E one octave below the bass-clef staff upwards for three octaves.

Tuning Fork. A two-pronged acoustical vibrator, made of steel, which produces a precise musical tone; it supplies a standard pitch for tuning musical instruments.

Tutti. The indication in an orchestral or choral score that the entire orchestra, or an entire chorus, is to enter; usually placed after an extended solo passage.

Twelve-Tone Music. A modern method of composition in which the principal theme, or *tone-row*, consists of twelve different notes, which in the course of the piece are rearranged in retrograde motion, inversion, and retrograde inversion; the same twelve notes underlie the horizontal contrapuntal lines and the vertical harmonic structure, resulting in a maximum concentration of thematic content.

Tympani. Common misspelling of Timpani.

Ukulele. A Hawaiian instrument having four strings, strummed with the fingertips.

Una corda. *see* Corda.

Unison. A single note or a melody line, played or sung by several performers at the same pitch or doubled one or more octaves apart, such as high and low voices singing the same melody. In orchestra and choral music, the abbreviation "unis." terminates a "divisi" passage (*see* Divisi).

Un poco. "A little;" as in *un poco più vivo* (a little more lively).

Upright Piano. A piano stood up vertically, with its strings arranged cross-wise (diagonally) along the vertical soundboard, as distinguished from a grand piano in which the strings and the soundboard are horizontal. *See also* Pedal.

Ut. French term for C.

Valse. French word for Waltz.

Variations. Elaborations of a theme, accomplished by a variety of means, such as multiple ornamentation profusely applied, with trills, arpeggios, passing notes, appoggiaturas, etc.; or by changing from the major key of a theme to a minor key (often marked *minore* for emphasis), or from the minor key of the theme to major (marked *maggiore*); or by using altogether different harmonies for the theme, and by changing the character and texture of the accompaniment, etc. Sometimes, variations depart so widely from the skeleton of the theme as to become almost independent compositions.

Veloce. Swift; with unremitting velocity.

Vibraphone. A percussion instrument consisting of suspended metal bars in keyboard arrangement, which, when struck with mallets, produce tones that are amplified by resonator tubes below the bars. A motor-driven mechanism causes the vibrato that gives the instrument its name.

Vibration. Rapid wave motion of a string or any other sound-producing medium. The greater the frequency of vibrations, the higher the sound produced.

Vibrato. A slight variation in pitch in string instruments, or a tremulant action of the vocal chords, to enhance the expressive quality of the sound.

Viol. A category of old, bowed string instruments, such as Tenor Viol or Bass Viol.

Viola. A bowed string instrument with its four strings tuned a fifth lower than the violin: C, G, D, A.

Viola da braccio. Literally, "viol for the arm." An old, bowed string instrument held in the arm, like the violin or viola.

Viola da gamba. Literally, "viol for the leg." An old, bowed string instrument of the size approximating the cello.

Violin. The highest bowed string instrument, with its four strings tuned in fifths: G, D, A, E.

Violoncello. A bowed string instrument, with its four strings, C, G, D, A, tuned one octave below the viola. The word actually means "little big violin." It is commonly called Cello.

Virginal. A small harpsichord, or a pair of small harpsichords built into a single box, widely known in the sixteenth and seventeenth centuries, especially in England. Also called Spinet.

Virtuoso. An artist possessing a superlative technique and consummate skill of performance.

Vivace. Vivacious, lively.

Vivo. Animated.

Vocal Score. An edition of a composition for voices with orchestra or chamber ensemble, in which the instrumental accompaniment has been arranged for piano. Most operas and oratorios are published in the form of vocal scores.

Voce. Voice; used in such phrases as *sotto voce* (in a subdued voice); *colla voce* (with the voice, that is, adjusting the accompaniment to the solo singer), etc.

Volta. Literally, "a turn;" used to indicate alternative bars or endings before the repeat sign, marked respectively *Prima volta* and *Seconda volta*.

Vorspiel. German word for a prelude or overture.

Waltz. A popular parlor dance in 3/4 time; also an instrumental composition, sometimes quite elaborate, in waltz time.

Well-Tempered Scale. *see* Tempered Scale.

Whole-Tone. A diatonic degree of two semitones.

Whole-Tone Scale. A melodic progression of six whole steps to an octave, lacking the dominant and major or minor tetrachords, and the sense of tonality; used in Impressionistic music to produce an atmosphere of exotic mystery.

Xylophone. Literally, "sounding wood." An instrument with wooden bars in keyboard arrangement, played with mallets.

Zarzuela. A Spanish operetta.

Zingarese. Gypsy. *Alla zingarese*, "in the manner of gypsy music."

Zither. A string instrument, popular in Central Europe, somewhat similar to an autoharp, placed on a table and plucked like a guitar or mandolin.

A Complete Index to
the New Scribner Music Library
by Composers

A Complete Index to
the New Scribner Music Library
by Titles

[131]

[137]